Streetwise® Start Your Own Business Workbook

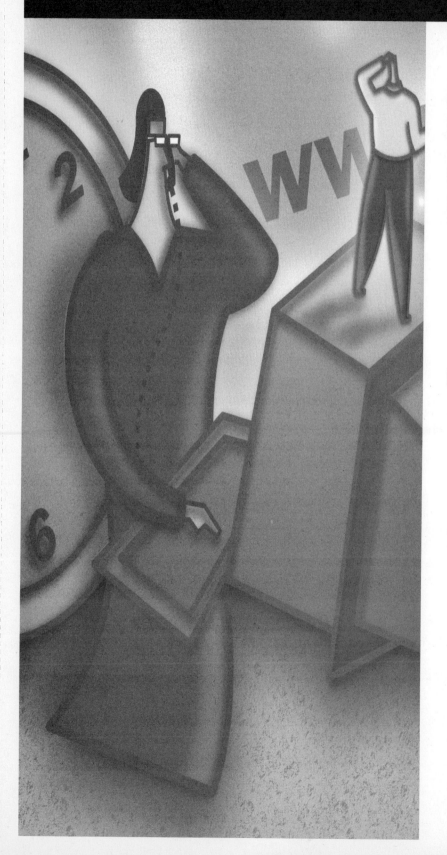

Worksheets, Forms, and Advice to Get Off on the Right Foot!

by Gina Marie Mangiamele

Adams Media Corporation
Avon, Massachusetts

A Streetwise® Publication.
Streetwise® is a registered trademark of Adams Media Corporation.

Published by Adams Media Corporation
57 Littlefield Street, Avon, MA 02322. U.S.A.
www.adamsmedia.com

ISBN: 1-58062-506-1

Printed in Canada.

J I H G F E D C B

Library of Congress Cataloging-in-Publication Data
Mangiamele, Gina Marie.
Streetwise start your own business workbook / by Gina Marie Mangiamele.
p. cm.
ISBN 1-58062-506-1
1. New business enterprises–Handbooks, manuals, etc.
2. Small business–Handbooks, manuals, etc. I. Title.
HD62.5 .M3553 2002
658.1'1–dc21

This publication is designed to provide accurate and authoritative information with regard to the subject matter covered. It is sold with the understanding that the publisher is not engaged in rendering legal, accounting, or other professional advice. If legal advice or other expert assistance is required, the services of a competent professional person should be sought.

–From a *Declaration of Principles* jointly adopted by a Committee of the American Bar Association and a Committee of Publishers and Associations

Cover illustration by Eric Mueller.

This book is available at quantity discounts for bulk purchases.
For information, call 1-800-872-5627.

Table of Contents

Acknowledgments

The author is grateful to the many individuals who were important to the completion of this publication. A special thanks is extended to my husband, Paul Mangiamele, for his never-ending patience, support, and encouragement. Many thanks to Adele, Mike, and Nana, and to everyone at Adams Media Corporation for the opportunity to write this workbook. Most important, the author is most appreciative of the efforts of Jere Calmes, former senior editor for Adams Media for his demonstrated support and confidence in this publication. Many, many thanks to everyone involved.

Introduction

Business ownership is a booming trend in the United States. People of all ages, ethnic groups, and socioeconomic backgrounds are challenging the odds and testing their business ideas in the marketplace. Since the mid-1980s, small business start-ups have been growing dramatically. The Small Business Administration's Office of Advocacy has reported that in 1999, 17.7 million Americans were self-employed as sole proprietorships, 1.8 million businesses were partnerships, and 5.3 million businesses were corporations. Small businesses (defined as 500 employees or fewer) employ 52 percent of private-sector workers, 51 percent of workers on public assistance, and 38 percent of workers in high-tech occupations. What you should understand from this data is that your business aspirations are consistent with those of thousands of other Americans. In the 1950s and '60s, achieving the American dream was represented by owning your own home. In the new millennium, the American dream could very well come to be represented by owning your own business.

Unfortunately, aspiring entrepreneurs are overwhelmed, don't understand the steps to starting a business, and are unsure of where to look for answers to their many questions. I've written this workbook to help you through the start-up process in a fun and comprehensive manner.

Streetwise® Start Your Own Business Workbook will provide you with step-by-step procedures for completing each important area of start-up. Forms, checklists, and question-driven formats offer you a means by which to organize your thoughts, ideas, and concepts and to translate them into action. Working with these simple, straightforward formats will make starting your own business a cinch! Completing the worksheets should also help you develop the confidence and assurance that your concept is a viable business venture.

Your investment of time and money to purchase this workbook should be rewarded by effective utilization of the information provided. Think of this publication as your personal business partner and road map to starting your business. Like true road maps, it will demonstrate a pointed direction and help you through this planning stage. The trick is to make use of the workbook and let it go to work for you.

If, for any reason, you have questions or comments related to the content of this book, you're invited and encouraged to send me your feedback in writing. I will respond to you whether you have a question, need clarification, or simply want to provide an opinion on the content. Interacting with me in this way may help support your entrepreneurial quest. Please send your correspondence to Gina Marie Mangiamele, c/o Adams Media Corporation, 57 Littlefield Street, Avon, MA 02322. Because you're reading the first edition of this workbook, your feedback is important to the quality of this publication. So please let me know your impression.

Review the workbook before you actually begin working in it. Start by leafing through each of the pages to get a sense of what I'm presenting and how it relates to your business start-up. You probably did this in the bookstore when you were deciding whether or not to make the purchase. Now take the time to give it a good review and approach the review with strategy in mind.

These pages have provided a specific documentation strategy for note taking and for retaining gathered information. Please try to embrace this strategy and see if it helps the process. Then review the table of contents and pick out sections you feel comfortable tackling first. This will help you get started and will encourage a proactive approach to following through on all planning stages. From there, you'll feel more confident about completing the remaining chapters in the workbook. Finally, as the pages become filled and you've stepped through the activities, you'll make a profound discovery that there has been progress and real results.

Baby Steps to Preparation

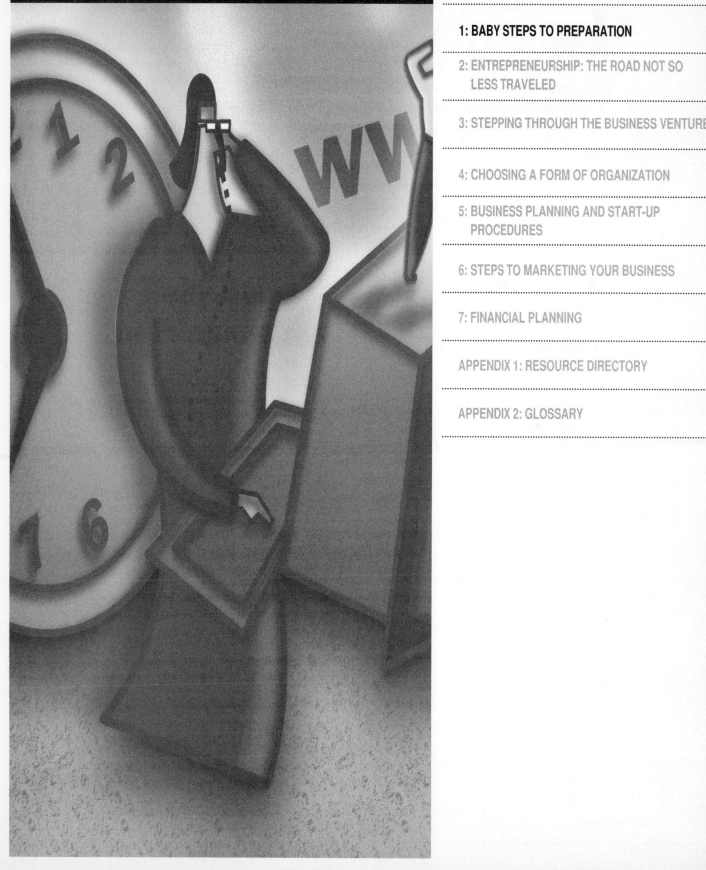

Chapter 1

Ideas float around in your head, keeping your brain active when you should be sleeping. It's hard to clear your mind because so many business concepts seem to clutter every thought. The ceiling in your bedroom has become a visual canvas for envisioning daily operations. Yet although every detail is clear in your own mind, perhaps you've never taken the time to write down any of your ideas for starting a business.

If opening your business is ever to be a reality, the documentation process will need to begin. Keeping all your plans in your mind is a dangerous practice. There's a chance that original ideas could be forgotten and important questions not get asked. For this reason, you need to create a safe haven for storing thoughts, creative concepts, contacts, and crucial information related to your business venture. Although *Streetwise® Start Your Own Business Workbook* is intended to lead you step by step through the process, developing a written bank of business information will be advantageous. Keeping notes on your ideas and working with this text will ensure that you pay adequate attention to each important aspect of launching a business provide you with step by step procedures for completing each important area of start-up.

Preparing a Bank of Business Information

Preparing your bank of business information begins with the purchase of a five-subject notebook. Here, you'll keep track of important information to be used when completing pages in this workbook.

Start by dividing the five-subject notebook into the categories outlined below.

Business Contacts

This section should contain the names, addresses, and communication information of everyone you come in contact with who could have an impact on your business start-up. Be sure to include a description of what they do and how you feel they could help you. Typically, these contacts could be chamber of commerce presidents, trade association members, economic development specialists, and government agencies.

Equipment and Supply Information

This section will be a vault for storing and organizing information concerning contacts, costs, delivery, terms, and other such data for those providing products or services to your business. Everything related to purchasing supplies, services, equipment, inventory, and anything you need for operations should be noted in this part of the notebook. After your business is up and running, you may choose to transfer this data to Rolodex cards or an electronic database.

You may be tempted to show off: to lease the corner office in a prestigious building and decorate it with designer furniture. Don't do it! It won't make you any money. And when your business is in a slow cycle, and you have angry creditors at your door, you'll wonder, "Did I spend just a little too much money on my office suite?"

For most small businesses, in fact, you're much better off running your business out of your home. Unless you're operating a retail store or expect clients to regularly visit your office, your face to the world will be your products, your services, your literature, and your marketing.

Running a business out of your home is increasingly well accepted. Be sure your business office looks professional and, if possible, arrange for a separate entrance. You can also always meet at your customer's location or, for a really image-conscious customer, you could even rent a meeting room.

Marketing Research

This section will contain information discovered at the library, in conversation, on Internet sites, or in publications. Having your notebook available at all times enables you to jot down tidbits of information, paste in news articles, write down Web site addresses, or note a book you should be reading as the information arises. Maintaining this section of the notebook will help you manage such data effectively.

Marketing Ideas

This section is the place to record those thoughts that may pop into your brain in the middle of the night, in a meeting, or at the most unexpected times. Use this section to keep track of everything that could become a part of your marketing and advertising plan. Here, you will paste ads from newspapers or tape business cards that have a great font, color, or style. I'm a strong believer in not reinventing the wheel. Pay attention to what others are doing and develop ideas from what's around you.

Questions and Answers

This section focuses on one of the most important aspects of the business start-up process–your questions. Use this section of the notebook to write down your questions when you think of them. Remember that every question is an important one that should be followed up on. If you're not sure of an answer, don't assume; instead, take the time to get the facts. Leave spaces between your questions in which to write down answers after you get them. This exercise will be the most worthwhile activity during your business start-up.

Finding Free Resources

Throughout the start-up process, be sure to take advantage of the many resources available to you, several of which are listed in this book's resource directory. Free and confidential business consulting, for example, is available through Small Business Development Centers (SBDC), which are sponsored by the U.S. Small Business Administration (SBA). Refer to the Web site at *www.adbdc-us.gov* for the location of the SBDC nearest you. The SBA also offers specialized support to women and minority entrepreneurs. See its Web site at *www.sba.gov.*

Establishing a Daily Agenda

Be sure to set a business start-up agenda for each day. Establish a to-do list and limit it to no more than five items per day. If you need to accomplish more than that in a day, delegate! It is far better to take a small step ahead each day, every day, than to overwhelm yourself with an impossible list of tasks that ultimately allows for nothing to be accomplished.

Use the following worksheet to help organize your daily start-up activities. Keep track of the time you start and end your day. Knowing the number of hours you invest each day will help you determine if you're just working hard or working smart. Use your time wisely and accomplish something every day.

Time and money are both important in business. Yet many businesspeople tend to give a lot more thought to how they spend their money than their time. Too often, how we spend our time is thought of only in terms of, "What am I going to do today?" or "What should I do next?"

Just as a well-run business should carefully develop a strategy to determine how to spend its money, an effective businessperson carefully develops a strategy to determine how to use his or her time. Just as a well-run business follows a budget in spending money, an effective businessperson follows a budget (or schedule) in spending time.

BUSINESS START-UP DAILY TO-DO'S

Day of the week: ____________________

Date: ____________________

Today's objective is to complete:

____

____

____

Starting time: ____________________

1. Respond to e-mail

To: ____________________ About: ____________________

To: ____________________ About: ____________________

To: ____________________ About: ____________________

To: ____________________ About: ____________________

(Modify your own form to include more, if needed, or eliminate if you don't use e-mail.)

2. Complete telephone calls.

Name/phone number: ____________________

Calling in reference to: ____________________

Name/phone number: ____________________

Calling in reference to: ____________________

Name/phone number: ____________________

Calling in reference to: ____________________

Name/phone number: ____________________

Calling in reference to: ____________________

Name/phone number: ____________________

Calling in reference to: ____________________

3. Complete business activities (to do list) Completed:

1) ________________ ❑

2) ________________ ❑

3) ________________ ❑

4) ________________ ❑

5) ________________ ❑

NOTES ON THE ABOVE:

The first step in effective time management is not to develop a schedule, but instead to develop a time strategy. The time strategy should be based on a short list of time priorities.

You start by identifying the number-one way you can most increase profits by using your time, and then identify the number-two way, the number-three way, and so on. This short list of time priorities forms the foundation of your time planning for every week of the year.

These time priorities may be identical to key parts of your company strategy, or they may be different. For example, if your company strategy is based on excellent customer service and you have a terrific customer service manager, spending lots of your time in customer service may not be the best use of your time.

Entrepreneurship: The Road Not So Less Traveled

Chapter 2

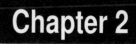

In years past, business ownership was thought to be a road traveled only by the very rich. It was a road less traveled for the average laborer until the dawn of corporate downsizing and the subsequent small- and home-based business explosion. As *Fortune* 500 corporations worked to beef-up the bottom line, increase efficiency, and compete globally, millions of workers across the country lost their jobs and discovered that self-employment was a viable alternative. With each passing year, entrepreneurship became the road not so less traveled.

Entrepreneurship requires an individual to possess a passion to succeed and a willingness to risk everything. Entrepreneurs are individuals who engage in the creative pursuit of an independent pathway that leads to self-employment. Courageous in their efforts, these determined leaders strive to manage their personal economic future while gaining independence. Entrepreneurs are people who understand the need to struggle and who will responsibly meet the challenge. The question is, are you an entrepreneur?

Assessing Your Skills and Attributes

Success as an entrepreneur hinges more on your mindset than on actual skill. While certain skills are absolutely necessary for business ownership, possessing the willingness to work long hours, accept risk and failure, be self-directed, and manage never-ending challenges are key components in creating a successful business enterprise. For each of the items in the following worksheet, rate yourself on a scale of one to five, with one being the lowest skill level and five being the greatest skill level.

ASSESSING YOUR SKILLS AND ATTRIBUTES

Rate your skill and ability to:					
Be creative	1	2	3	4	5
Be patient	1	2	3	4	5
Listen	1	2	3	4	5
Accept good advice	1	2	3	4	5
Manage many tasks	1	2	3	4	5
Make good decisions	1	2	3	4	5
Continue to learn	1	2	3	4	5
Utilize resources	1	2	3	4	5
Ask for help	1	2	3	4	5
Communicate	1	2	3	4	5

Scoring mostly fives indicates that you possess the skills necessary to get along with people and use the resources and opportunities available to create a successful business. If you scored a mix of ones, twos, and threes, figure out how to strengthen those weaknesses. Remember that with any new job, growing into a new position is all a part of the process. The same is true for business ownership. The longer you work at it the better you'll get.

Assessing Your Personality

To establish a basis of how entrepreneurial you are today, complete the following quiz. When you're finished, add up your score and determine whether you have the potential to be successful as a business owner.

BUSINESS OWNERSHIP QUIZ

1. How many businesses of your own have you opened?

a. Two or more	10 points
b. One	7 points
c. None	0 points

2. Why do you want to open your own business?

a. To build personal wealth	3 points
b. To eliminate employers	10 points
c. To gain public recognition	0 points

3. While growing up, was your home environment . . .

a. Stressful	7 points
b. Cozy	2 points
c. Highly competitive	10 points

4. When tough decisions need to be made you . . .

a. Search for resources and help	10 points
b. Take a long time to decide	0 points
c. Reach decisions without seeking advice	5 points

5. You can get really excited over . . .

a. New products	3 points
b. Crazy new ideas	5 points
c. Both of the above	10 points

Total score: ________

If you scored thirty-five points or above, you possess a natural ability to be a business owner. While this exercise is brief, it does give you an overview of the personality characteristics favorable to entrepreneurship.

Take some time to address the questions in the following worksheet. These questions require some honest soul searching. Ask your family members (who probably know you best) to voice opinions and offer examples.

PERSONALITY CHARACTERISTICS

1. Are you a self-directed, highly motivated individual?
   ❑ Yes ❑ No
2. Can you tolerate different points of view?
   ❑ Yes ❑ No
3. Can you be persuasive?
   ❑ Yes ❑ No
4. Are you known as someone who always gets along with others?
   ❑ Yes ❑ No
5. Do you get along with your family?
   ❑ Yes ❑ No
6. Are you compulsive about being organized and neat?
   ❑ Yes ❑ No
7. Can you work long hours and function on little sleep?
   ❑ Yes ❑ No
8. Are you an education junkie, always looking for new resources, information, and opportunities to learn?
   ❑ Yes ❑ No
9. For you, is the glass half full, and do you try to find a way to fill it up?
   ❑ Yes ❑ No
10. Do you want to start your own business?
    ❑ Yes ❑ No

Stepping through this activity should have provided you with increased awareness of your personal attributes and your likelihood of success as a business owner. While this simple quiz isn't the end-all for deciding whether you should begin a business, it does offer a basis for judging your own capabilities. After all, your success and the tools you use to achieve that success are your decision and responsibility. Being honest and responsive may enhance your chances for long-term growth and ongoing success.

Too often, we tend to think of efficiency as something relegated to the production process. But with so much of today's work being done in offices, not factories, there's a lot to be gained from focusing on efficiency in cubicles. Consider taking specific steps like implementing a two-hour morning quiet time and encouraging cross-functional interaction at all levels.

Deciding Why You Want to Start a Business

In the following worksheet, expand on the last question in the preceding worksheet by writing down specific reasons why you desire business ownership.

TOP TEN REASONS FOR STARTING A BUSINESS

1. ______________________________
2. ______________________________
3. ______________________________
4. ______________________________
5. ______________________________
6. ______________________________
7. ______________________________
8. ______________________________
9. ______________________________
10. ______________________________

Put these reasons in a place where you will see them every day. You may have many days when you ask yourself why you started this venture. Reading your own list of reasons will serve as a reminder and a motivator for you to keep going and triumph over the tough challenges of your entrepreneurial journey.

Knowing What's Involved

The following chapters help you make decisions and take important steps toward starting a business. As you go through each of the remaining chapters in this workbook, indicate on the following worksheet that you've taken (or will take) these steps.

START-UP STEPS CHECKLIST AND PROGRESS REPORT

Description	Date Completed	Will Be Done By
Completed personal assessment		
Completed business assessment		
Assessed assets		
Chose form of organization		
Filed d.b.a. or other form		
Created a mission statement		
Defined an industry gap		
Developed product or service		
Completed market research		
Identified customer base		
Did competitive analysis		
Did location analysis		
Determined a location		
Secured lease or purchase		
Handled zoning/ local law issues		
Purchased supplies		
Purchased inventory		
Purchased equipment and fixtures		
Created personnel requirements		
Identified bookkeeping system		
Secured professionals		
Created eight-point marketing plan		
Prepared assumptions		
Projected income/expenses		
Projected cash flow		
Completed break-even analysis		
Created inception balance sheet		
Obtained a credit history		
Secured capital/loans		
Opened operating accounts		
Purchased insurance		
Obtained telephone service		
Obtained utility services		
Purchased signage		
Planned grand opening		
Other event: ______________		
Other event: ______________		

Stepping Through the Business Venture

Chapter 3

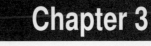

Creativity is the source of innovative ideas, solutions to problems, and new ways to think about current situations. Creativity is the essential ingredient that enables freethinking and an "anything goes" attitude. Your business venture needs both creativity and a process for applying your thoughts. In this chapter, you'll use your creativity to guide the process of thinking through your venture.

Knowledge is the basis for thought. Basic information must be acquired before opinions or conclusions can be drawn. When thinking through your business venture, remember to utilize the knowledge you've already acquired and seek out missing data. The combination of the two will act as a foundation for creating business strategies.

Five Basic Types of Business Knowledge

General Industry Knowledge

General industry knowledge refers to your understanding of the industry as it stands today. It's obtained by reading newspapers and magazines, listening to the television and radio, and hearing the opinions of others about the industry. Your general industry knowledge should be one of the reasons you've decided to enter into a particular type of business enterprise.

Business Operations Knowledge

Business operations knowledge can be described as your skill set for business management. Understanding the industry alone will not help you manage a profitable business. Knowledge of marketing, cash flow, accounts payable, accounts receivable, purchasing, and other operational areas will be necessary for you to make decisions, respond to new and changing market trends, and coordinate business activities to meet company goals.

Knowledge of Current Market Opportunities

Knowledge of current market opportunities refers to your ability to identify those customers in your geographic area who will want to pay for your product or service. Time must be spent gathering information to identify the market. Resources and tools are available to help you locate this information. Local chambers of commerce, town halls, and public libraries may offer studies, reports, and census information that provide the answers you're looking for. Market research groups can also compile this information for a fee; however, much of it can be obtained from various sources free of charge. For example, your local government may have a GIS (Geographic Information Survey) report available at no cost. The GIS report is a graphic map of your local business area showing various demographic information within a one-, three-, or five-mile ring. This information may include income ranges, ethnic breakdown, number of households and so on.

A lot of companies are spending money to build elaborate Web sites only to be frustrated with the small amount of revenue their sites are generating. Despite the so-called success stories you read about, few companies are making money on their Web sites.

If you're considering a Web site for your firm, take an incremental approach. Start with a simple site and gradually expand it, keeping careful track of your revenue, your costs, and how much your current customers are using the site.

Even a small business today should consider a simple Web site. Keep the graphics simple, but have a few paragraphs of text that explain what your business does and why prospects should do business with you instead of your competition.

Even without programming skills, you can create basic Web pages yourself using off-the-shelf software. Your only ongoing cost will be about $50 a month to an Internet service provider.

Unique and Specific Venture Knowledge

Unique and specific venture knowledge relates to the type of business you'll start. Will you be a retailer, wholesaler, manufacturer, or service provider? Depending on your choice, you'll need to know which licenses, permits, or certificates may be required. To acquire venture-specific knowledge means you'll need to seek out specific, detailed information concerning legal and regulatory requirements, zoning, and operational and other prerequisites required for your venture.

Knowledge of Industry Gaps and Voids

Knowledge of industry gaps and voids requires the discovery of a flaw or problem within the industry. Usually the industry gap directly identifies a "black hole" of customer needs that are not currently being met. Scrutinizing the voids in the industry will prompt the creation of new approaches to address each customer's needs. Finding out what pains the customer is where you'll find the gap. Successfully filling the gap translates into money for you and your business.

So much of communicating successfully is listening successfully. Even if you don't listen well, you can learn to do it better. When an employee or client has a problem, listen to the person's perspective and then paraphrase it back to them. This way, the person knows you understand what he or she said and that you care about the problem.

Documenting Your Knowledge of the Industry

So how much knowledge do you have? Compiling your creative thoughts, documenting your five areas of knowledge, and utilizing this information to create industry assumptions will ultimately set the pathway for your business plan.

INDUSTRY KNOWLEDGE

1. Your general industry knowledge:
   a. What is the specific industry you will operate in?

   b. Describe your specific industry knowledge.

   c. What new technologies are impacting trends in this industry?

   d. What are the top five issues related to this industry?

   e. Who are the big competitive players in this industry?

2. Your business operations knowledge:
   a. List prior business operations involvement.

b. List the most recent classes you've attended on business plan development, taxes, accounting, bookkeeping, marketing, financial analysis, sales, and strategic planning. Include the dates that you took each class.

c. What accounting method will you use?
Cash basis or accrual?

Manual ledger or automated system?

Internal handling or outsourced services?

d. Who will be your professionals of record?

Banker:

Accountant:

Insurance agent:

Lawyer:

Business adviser(s):

Industry trade professional:

Financial adviser:

e. What agencies do you know about that could serve as ongoing resources to the business?

f. What will be the chain of command for the business?

3. Your market opportunities knowledge:
   a. What are the primary opportunities you've identified in this industry?

   b. What factors in the marketplace will be the biggest challenges?

c. What is the life expectancy of your product or service?

d. What percentage of market share do you expect to capture?

e. How long will it take to achieve market share?

f. Who will be your competitors?

4. Your unique and specific knowledge about this industry:
   a. What government agencies regulate this industry?

   b. Are there sales tax requirements? ❑ Yes ❑ No
   If yes, have you obtained the applications to collect sales tax? ❑ Yes ❑ No

   c. Is zoning approval required? ❑ Yes ❑ No

   d. Is signage approval required? ❑ Yes ❑ No

   e. If your business will be home based, will the town require a home-based business permit? ❑ Yes ❑ No

f. Is a special insurance policy needed? ❑ Yes ❑ No
If yes, what policies do you need?

g. What trade publications are in print on the industry? (List existing publications in your notebook with the addresses, Web sites, and e-mail information.)

h. Does a local trade organization assist business owners with regulatory requirements and business operational issues? (For example, the Palm Beach Restaurant Association is a resource for local restaurant owners. List these organizations in your notebook. Obtain membership information for each group identified.)

5. Your knowledge of industry gaps and voids:
   a. What pains the customer about this industry?

   b. List five key problems the competitors have not addressed in this industry. (For example, wasting half the day waiting for the cable TV guy to show up is a common complaint of cable service consumers.)

   c. What will resolve these industry issues? What are your specific solutions?

d. Assuming you can't be all things to all people, define what segment of the solution your business will address.

e. To conclude this section, review your responses and creatively compile an opinion and some conclusions about the industry.

What are the pros and cons?

How will deficiencies in any of the knowledge areas be addressed?

What areas are strength areas?

What else needs to be considered? In what way could you think about the venture from an entirely different perspective?

What do others say about your opinions and conclusions? What do they think about your business ideas?

Whether your business is a one-person start-up or a huge corporation, a great strategy is crucial. It's like the steering wheel on a ship. If the ship is in A-1 condition except for a broken steering wheel, it's going to spin hopelessly in circles.

Try a complete strategic review with your key employees. At the very least, discuss the following: future vision (what kind of company do you want in five years), strengths, weaknesses, markets (what opportunities and challenges loom ahead), strategic options (what are your basic alternatives), selection, and implementation.

Gathering Industry Information

Gathering information about a particular industry is often a bewildering assignment for entrepreneurs. Experience is often a good teacher, and entrepreneurs frequently can readily provide a good general description of an industry simply because they have been a part of it. However, for the purposes of a business plan, more specific and quantifiable information is often needed. Frequently, this requires that you consult industry or company observers; review published sources, either printed or electronic; or utilize one of the many available industry databases.

As you begin to gather industry data, make a list of possible industry contacts or industry participants. These may include people and companies that are part of the channel of distribution, industry observers, or service organizations. If you are new to the industry you will need to seek out these individuals. A short listing of the type of people you might consult appears in Table 3-1:

TABLE 3-1

Potential Consultants Channel Members	Industry Observers	Service Organizations
Suppliers	Bankers	Trade associations
Distributors	Auditors/accountants	Chambers of commerce
Customers	Regulators	Trade conventions
Advertising agencies	Stockbrokers	Centers for business research
Market researchers	Industry experts	Franchisers
Media firms	Universities	
Competitors		

You may be surprised to see competitors listed among the potential sources for you to contact. It would seem natural that competitors would be quite unwilling to cooperate and supply information given the potential for conflict of interest. Yet depending on the nature of your questions and the competitive situation within your industry, this may not be the case. This especially holds true in the context of small business. Some companies that you might assume are competitors may not see themselves that way because they may, for example, serve a different geographic market or a different segment of the market. Further, small business owners often recall clearly the difficulties they had getting started and will take fledgling firms "under their wing."

Industry experts represent a source of information that is often overlooked. An index of these experts is published by Washington researchers in a book titled *Who Knows What: A Guide to the Experts* (1995). These individuals spend their professional lives studying and tracking the events within specific industries. Many times they will share their knowledge with a small business owner (with a well-organized list of questions) or can direct you to articles or publications they may have authored.

Frequently, industry observers such as bankers, consultants, and stockbrokers are restricted by confidentiality and professional guidelines as to what they may disclose. However, you can ask for an interview, request industry reports, and solicit recommendations for other sources to consult. Very often these firms and individuals can disclose general, but still significant, industry trends and upcoming events without compromising confidential information about specific companies.

Entrepreneurs often overlook trade associations in their search for industry data, yet they represent a rich source of information about their industries. After all, they exist to serve the business, technical, and informational needs of their membership. Most industries have trade associations that act as clearinghouses for industry data. Some even publish very detailed industry statistics. Trade associations are also normally involved in tracking and evaluating pending industry governmental regulations. They can be of great assistance in helping to identify published materials, recommending industry experts, describing industry structures, and explaining key industry trends. Very often trade associations will provide assistance to new firms in hopes that the firm will later consider membership in the organization. Two excellent sources of information on trade associations include *The Encyclopedia of Associations, International Organizations* and *Small Business Source Book* from the Gale Group, 1999.

You can also find tremendous amounts of information on an industry both in printed material and online. Too often, small business owners assume that published material only exists relative to large businesses. There are many sources available, the problem is finding them. An excellent place to start is in the business holdings section of your local college or public library. Reference librarians will normally welcome the opportunity to be of assistance. Industry publications often quote experts, cite other published works, and refer to leaders in the industry.

If you have access to the Internet, you will find a wide variety of resources to assist you in your research. Many trade associations, business publications, governmental agencies, and research companies publish information on the Internet, in full or in abstract form. Unfortunately, much of the information on the Internet is stored rather unsystematically. Your patience and determination will be rewarded.

Use the following worksheets to keep a record of the information you find.

YOUR INDUSTRY

1. Describe the primary industry of which your business is a part.

2. What Standard Industrial Classification (SIC) code(s) apply to your business?

3. What is the current status of the industry based on each of the following?

   Sales trends ($ and units):

   Growth rates:

4. Is the number of competitors increasing, decreasing or staying the same?

5. Why?

6. How is the industry affected by changes in the economy in any of the following areas?

   Unemployment:

   Interest rates:

Inflation: ____________________

____

Profitability: ____________________

Consumer confidence: ____________________

____

7. When and how do seasonal factors impact industry sales?
   Christmas/other holidays:

   ____

   Summer/winter:

   ____

   Out of school/back to school:

   ____

   Other:

   ____

   ____

8. Which federal and/or state agencies regulate or oversee your industry and what impact do they have?
   OSHA: ____________________

   ____

   Food and Drug Administration (FDA): ____________________

   ____

   Environmental Protection Agency (EPA): ____________________

   ____

Department of Transportation (DOT):

Securities and Exchange Commission (SEC):

Bureau of Alcohol, Tobacco, and Firearms (ATF):

Other:

9. Are there any new products or product developments that could affect the industry or your venture?

10. Are there any new entrants, departures, or mergers?

11. Are there any new markets or customers who could affect the industry or your venture?

INDUSTRY FINANCIAL BENCHMARKS

1. Industry percentages of sales price attributable to:
   - Cost of materials ______%
   - Cost of labor ______%
   - Cost of sales ______%
   - Fixed cost/overhead ______%
   - Distribution costs ______%
   - Cost of goods sold ______%
   - Profit before interest and taxes ______%
   - Profit ______%

2. What are the financial averages in your industry

   Acid test ratio: (cash + receivables + marketable securities) ÷ current liabilities

   ____

   Quick ratio: (current assets – inventory) ÷ current liabilities

   ____

   - Accounts receivable as a percentage of total assets: ______%
   - Inventory as a percentage of total assets: ______%
   - Gross profit as a percentage of sales: ______%
   - Net profit (after tax) as a percentage of sales: ______%
   - Bad debt as a percentage of sales: ______%
   - Average collection period in days: ______
   - Return on assets: ______%
   - Return on investment: ______%
   - Inventory turnover rate: ______
   - Average wholesale markup: ______%
   - Average retail markup: ______%

3. Normal credit terms: ______ ______%

4. Other: ______ ______%

Seeking Outside Opinions

Hosting a forum of objective individuals to discuss your business ideas is a good practice. Seek out industry professionals, potential customers, legal and accounting professionals, and local economic development and planning professionals. After the roster of participants has been established, you'll need to develop the agenda for the forum. Following is a list of what to include in your meeting agenda:

1. List meeting day and date
2. List meeting time
3. List the names of the participants, their occupations and businesses.
4. Welcome the forum participants and introduce yourself.
5. Introduce the business concept. At this time, you'll speak about the purpose of the forum. Be prepared with a written narrative.
6. Introduce the participants. Each member of the forum should introduce him- or herself to the rest of the group. Limit the information to name, business, and occupation.
7. Distribute a list of forum questions to the participants.
8. Begin discussion.

Please note that someone should be responsible for taking notes and recording comments. If the group is agreeable, perhaps the session could be tape-recorded or video recorded. After the forum is over, go over the data and consider all the comments. This may help you reach some final decisions concerning the business start-up.

Sizing Up Your Competition

One of the stark realities of operating a business of any size is that you will face competition on a daily basis. It is not enough that there will be direct competitors (businesses similar to yours) but you will also face indirect competition (businesses not engaged in the same line of business as yours but that compete for the same dollars). Professional sports teams scout their opponents and devise game plans to exploit their opponents' weaknesses and avoid their strengths. You should scout your competition as well.

Prior to starting a new business or entering a new market, it is especially important for you to gain a strong handle on competitors' strengths and weaknesses, the products and services they offer, and the markets they serve. This should provide you with valuable insight into strategies you can use to capture your share of the market. In addition, this competitive research will give you the information you will need to provide a well-informed and reasoned response to your banker's inevitable question, "Who is your competition?" A thorough examination of the competitive environment you are contemplating entering should also be an important factor in your evaluation of your business's feasibility.

Plan to keep an eye on new entrants to your marketplace, both from within and outside of your industry. If new competitors are entering the market, it probably means they have identified an unserved or underserved market or a competitive weakness in the group of existing companies, including yours. By thoroughly researching new competitors and their intended strategies you may describe weaknesses in your operation that you had previously not been aware of, and you will be able to develop strategies to counteract new competitors.

Every business is strongly advised to develop an ongoing competitive intelligence program. It provides an inexpensive and forward-looking mechanism for protecting your business and your markets. It allows you to stay ahead of your competition and to quickly react to their competitive moves. One method of doing this is to establish competitor files or competitive scrapbooks. Every time you run across information about your competition, whether news articles, advertisements, tips from colleagues, or pieces of competitors' marketing literature, add it to the file. Periodically examining the file's contents can give you insight into competitors' strategies, target markets, patterns, and perhaps weaknesses, which you can use to plan your strategies.

The goal of your competitive data collection process is to compile as much company-specific information as possible. Given the lack of formal financial reporting requirements to which small businesses are subject, however, this is not always easily accomplished. It is more likely that you will have to resort to several observational methods to uncover the information you are seeking. Some suggested ways to accumulate information on your competition include:

- Visit their Web sites to observe the products and services they offer and to acquire company-specific background information.
- Shop their store or business location. Purchase an item or two, noting what credit cards they accept. Do they take checks? Are their people courteous, knowledgeable, and competent? What about return policies?
- Ask suppliers about them. Be careful here, because at some point they may ask the supplier about you.
- Check them out through Dun & Bradstreet, your local chamber of commerce, the Better Business Bureau, and similar organizations.
- Observe the kinds of customers who frequent the store or service and make note of when the business appears the busiest.

Regardless of how you choose to conduct competitive intelligence, it is extremely important that you do so. At the very least, you will have learned something about the arena you will compete in. At best, this activity will provide you with tremendous insight into how to position your business and the strategies that will be most effective for you to pursue. Use the following worksheets to keep a record of your findings.

ASSESSING THE COMPETITIVE LANDSCAPE

1. Which competitors have been the leaders in your market?

2. Which competitors have increased in size or market share substantially in the last two or three years?

3. Describe the general competitive trends in your market/industry.

4. Which competitor(s) do you plan to be most like? In what ways?

5. For each of your five closest competitors, complete the following:

Name	Location	How Long in Business?

6. For each of your three primary competitors, describe their strengths or competitive advantages:

Competitor	Strengths/Advantages

7. For the same competitors, describe their most significant weaknesses or competitive vulnerabilities:

Competitor	Weaknesses/Vulnerabilities

8. Identify products/services that may act as substitutes or alternatives (indirect competitors) to your own.

9. Compare competing products/services to your own based on the following:

Criteria	Your Product/Service	Your Competitors
Quality		
Customer appeal		
Customer awareness		
Customer satisfaction		
Customer support		
Delivery		
Service quality		
Warranties		
Other:		

LOOKING FORWARD

1. Name and describe potential future direct competitors.

2. Name and describe potential future indirect competitors.

3. Describe the competitive intelligence activities you will employ to stay abreast of the competition's strategies and actions.

4. Describe current competitors' likely reactions to your entry into the marketplace.

5. Name any current competitors that may be considering leaving the market.

COMPETITIVE COMPARISON MATRIX

For each of the evaluative criteria, assign a rating to your firm as well as to your competition. In the first column, rate the attribute from one to five based on its importance to your target market–five being most important to your customers and one being unimportant. In the columns designated for your company and for your competitors, rank your/their performance in each category from one to five, with five indicating that customer expectations were far exceeded and one indicating that performance falls far short of customer expectations.

FACTOR	IMPORTANCE TO CUSTOMER	YOUR COMPANY	COMPETITOR 1	COMPETITOR 2
Product/service features				
Pricing				
Discount sales				
Product quality				
Durability				
Convenience				
Name brands				
Reputation				
Warrantees				
Location				
Customer service				
Delivery time				
Knowledgeable salespeople				

FACTOR	IMPORTANCE TO CUSTOMER	YOUR COMPANY	COMPETITOR 1	COMPETITOR 2
Hours of operation				
Return policies				
Atmosphere				
Other:				
Total points				

COMPARING ORGANIZATIONAL STRENGTHS

You also want to rate yourself and your competitors on organizational factors. Use a scale of one to five, with five meaning extremely strong and one representing very weak.

FACTOR	YOUR COMPANY	COMPETITOR 1	COMPETITOR 2
Financial strength/resources			
Market acceptance			
Market penetration			
Product line			
Location(s)			
Competent sales force			
Management strength			
Workforce			

Factor	Your Company	Competitor 1	Competitor 2
Reputation in trade			
Reputation in community			
Promotional ability			
Name recognition			
Use of technology			
Innovativeness			
Marketing effectiveness			
Partnership/affiliations			
Supplier resources			
Patents/trademarks			
Other:			
Total points			

Choosing a Form of Organization

Chapter 4

Imagine that you're in a courtroom on the final day of your trial, waiting to hear the verdict in a liability case against you or your company. The near-empty courtroom is quiet, tension is mounting, and you feel anxious, short of breath, and nervous. Your attorney is silent with no words of encouragement.

Getting the picture? Now imagine that the verdict reads, "Judgment is for the plaintiff in the amount of $6,553,234.15." Now read the dollar amount again, only this time read it aloud so you can hear how it sounds and imagine that you owe the person or business that's suing you every dime of that amount. The very thought of a lawsuit is frightening enough, much less the thought of having to pay an unbelievable amount of money in damages. Protecting your personal and business assets against a lawsuit is a primary reason to carefully consider the form of organization you need for starting your business.

All too often, new entrepreneurs jump to the decision to become a sole proprietor and file a d.b.a. (doing business as) certificate because it's easy, inexpensive, and in many cases, believed to be the only option available to a new small business owner. In truth, there are many options for you as a start-up entrepreneur.

Assessing Your Assets

Before choosing the most appropriate form of organization for your business, you must determine which of your assets could be at risk and at what level you want to protect those assets. You must also consider your long-range plans for the business, as you may want to structure the organization for growth and, possibly, new investors.

Use the following worksheet to assess your assets. Try to include everything you own, from cash to collectibles.

PERSONAL ASSETS LIST

TYPE OF ASSET	TOTAL CURRENT BALANCE/VALUE
CASH ACCOUNTS	
Household checking account:	
Household savings account:	
Personal savings account:	
Total of all cash accounts:	
INVESTMENT ACCOUNTS	
Money market accounts:	
Mutual fund accounts:	
Stocks and bonds:	
Certificates of deposit:	
Treasury bills:	
Other investment accounts:	
Total of all investment accounts:	
REAL ESTATE	
Single-dwelling residence:	
Vacation property/summer home:	
Other real estate:	
Total of all real estate:	
VEHICLES (LIST MAKE AND YEAR)	
Vehicle #1:	
Vehicle #2:	
Boat:	
Other vehicle:	
Total of all vehicles:	
FURNITURE, FIXTURES, AND HOUSEHOLD ITEMS	
Appliances:	
Bookcases, tables, stands:	
Collectibles:	
Carpets, linens, wall hangings:	
Cookware, dishes, and utensils:	
Furniture (total of all):	
Lawn furniture and accessories:	

TYPE OF ASSET	TOTAL CURRENT BALANCE/VALUE
FURNITURE, FIXTURES, AND HOUSEHOLD ITEMS (CONTINUED)	
Musical instruments:	
Other:	
Total furniture and fixtures:	
EQUIPMENT	
Compressor:	
Lawn mower/lawn tools:	
Tools:	
Personal computer/printer:	
Copier:	
Fax:	
Telephones/cell/beepers:	
Other:	
Total of all equipment:	
RECREATIONAL EQUIPMENT	
Bicycles/sporting goods:	
Games and toys:	
Videos, CDs, DVDs:	
Total of all recreational equipment:	
OTHER REMAINING ASSETS	
Other:	
Other:	
Total of other assets:	
TOTAL FOR EACH CATEGORY	
Cash accounts:	$
Investment accounts:	$
Real estate:	$
Vehicles:	$
Furniture, fixtures, and houshold items	$
Equipment:	$
Recreational equipment:	$
Other remaining assets:	$
Total value of assets at risk:	$

You have now identified the assets that could be lost in the event of a lawsuit and have established the need to determine the most protective form of organization for your business. The next step is to consider the different forms of organization and their liabilities.

Sole Proprietor

Individuals may operate a business and process business transactions using their own birth name and personal social security number. There is no requirement to use a business name. Consultants, tutors, motivational speakers, and independent service providers like home health aids and nurses can easily operate without a business name. In doing so, these individuals are sole proprietors. If they choose to do business under a name other than their own, they must file a d.b.a. (doing business as) with the county clerk's office. The function of the filing is to disclose to the residents of the county that an individual living in the county is using a name other than his or her own for business purposes. For this reason, the d.b.a. is announced in local newspapers.

Liability for unsecured debt or for accidental death or injury and financial matters remain with the individual. Personal responsibility is imposed on the business owner because there is no separation of business and personal affairs. The liability exposure is 100 percent. Insurance may help to mitigate some of the risk; however, as a sole proprietor, the risk presented by a lawsuit could be great.

On the other hand, there are benefits to operating as a d.b.a. sole proprietor. First, organizing is easy and inexpensive. The filing at the county clerk's office can take less than an hour, and the fee is usually $25 for the filing fee, $4 for a certified copy of your business certificate, and $1 for the cost of the form. The certified copy of your d.b.a. is usually used to verify the filing to the bank when you open your business accounts.

Taxes required for a d.b.a. sole proprietorship include self-employment taxes, federal income taxes, and state income taxes (depending on your state). Taxes are calculated at the individual's tax rate, unlike a C-corporation, which has its own corporate tax rate.

Corporation

Organizing as a corporation, either as a C or as a subchapter S, will separate your personal assets from the business's assets. Think of a corporation as an artificial individual that can generate income, purchase goods and services, and perform other business functions. As a separate entity, the corporation provides a veil of protection for the business owner. Instead of a lawsuit being initiated against you as the business owner, it would be initiated against the corporation. Additionally, the common stock in a corporation may be sold, transferred, and willed. Although it's more expensive to file as a corporation, the structure, liability protection, and transferability of a corporation make this form of organization a viable option.

Limited Liability Company

Beginning with Wyoming in 1977, LLC laws have been passed in every state in the United States. The function of the LLC is to provide entity options to traditional corporations, limited partnerships, and general partnerships. Usually, an LLC requires at least two members; however, all states except two allow a sole owner LLC. The advantages are that double taxation is eliminated, income passes through to the member's personal tax return, and there is flexibility in the management of the organization. The greatest advantages are that liability is limited to the organization and that there may be an unlimited number of invested members. For entrepreneurs who are considering a general partnership, the LLC offers a means by which to mitigate risk. Because LLC laws vary from state to state, research your state laws for details. If you have Internet access, try using a search engine to locate detailed information on LLCs. Business Web sites often have articles on the subject, as will your state's Web site.

To help you size up the options, see the following chart.

TYPES OF COMPANIES

	Sole Proprietorship	Sub-Chapter S Corporation	C Corporation	Limited Liability Company
Liability	Owner of the business must carry 100 percent of the liability. There is no separation of personal assets from business assets. All unsecured debt is the responsibility of the owner. In a lawsuit, the owner is 100 percent responsible.	Owners have limited liability because the business assets are separate from the personal assets of the owner(s). All unsecured debt is the responsibility of the corporation unless personal guarantees were established.	Owners have limited liability because the business assets are separate from the personal assets of the owner(s). All unsecured debt is the responsibility of the corporation, unless personal guarantees were established.	Owners are called members. Liability is limited because assets of the business are separate from the owner's personal assets. Any entity may be a member of an LLC.
Transferability	No transferability of ownership.	Owner(s) have common stock that may be sold, transferred, or willed. or willed.	Owner(s) have common stock that may be sold, transferred,	Memberships in an LLC may be sold, transferred, or willed.
Set-Up	Easy to form and recordkeeping	Filing is done through the state government, usually the Dept. of State.	Filing is done through the state government, usually the Dept. of State.	Filing is done through the state government, usually the Dept. of State.
Taxation	Flow-through taxation: The owner files a Section C at the end of the year. Business income is taxed at the individual rate.	Flow-through taxation: Business income is taxed at the individual tax rate.	C corporations file their own tax returns and pay a corporate tax rate.	Flow-through taxation: Business income is taxed at the individual tax rate.
Ownership	One owner.	May have one to seventy-five owners who are also stockholders. Owners must be U.S. citizens/state residents.	May have two or more owners.	May have an unlimited number of members. Owners do not need to be U.S. citizens.
Fees	May file a d.b.a. certificate with the local county clerk's office. Costs are usually around $30.	Fees for filing a sub-S corporation vary from state to state.	Fees for filing a C corporation vary from state to state.	Fees for filing vary from state to state.
Legal	Check with your local county clerk's office for details on sole proprietorships in your area.	It is advised to use an attorney for this filing.	It is advised to use an attorney for this filing.	Check out the resources at *www.llcweb.com.*

Business Planning and Start-Up Procedures

Chapter 5

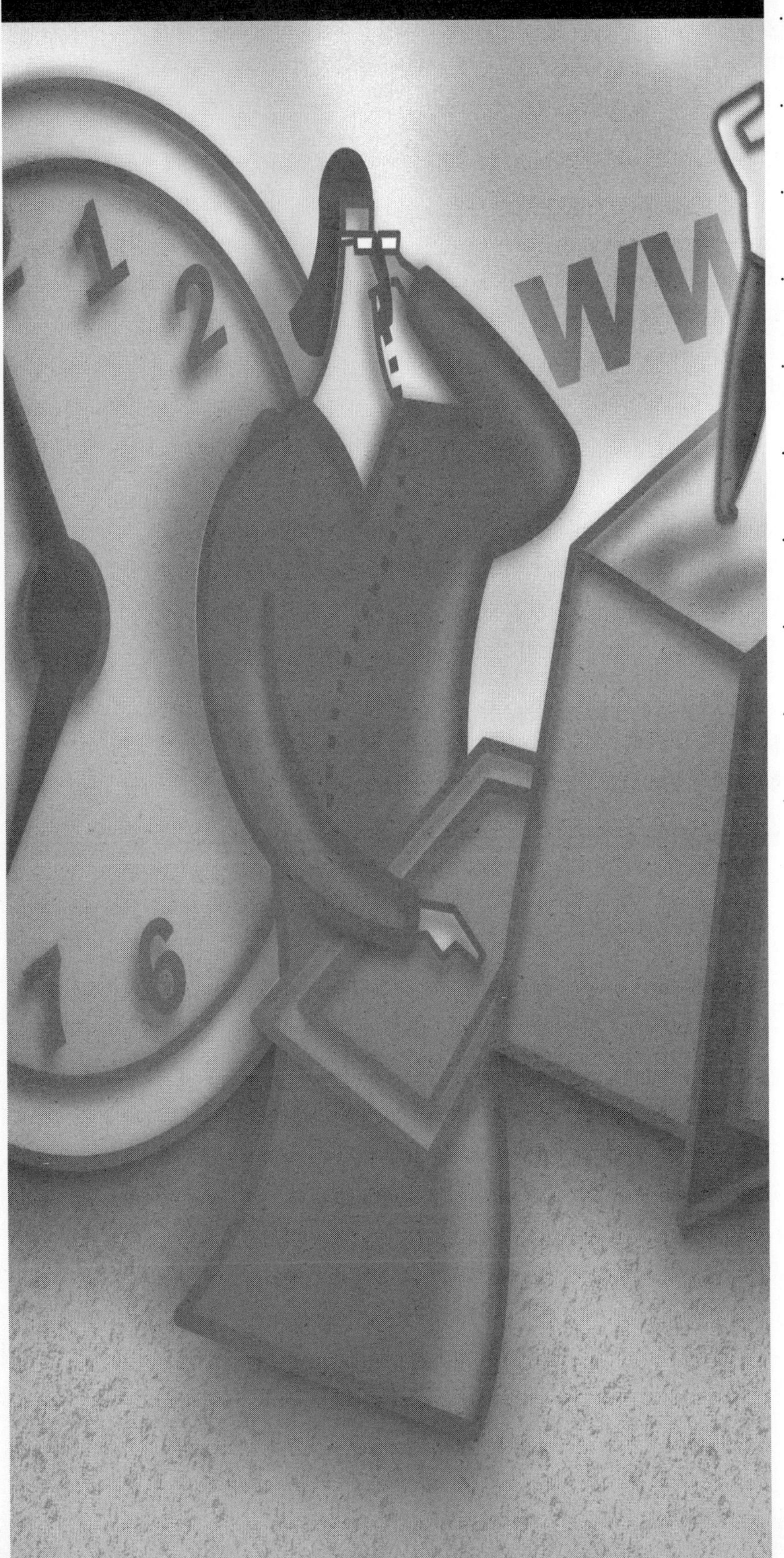

The heart and pulse of your business begins with completing a comprehensive business plan and initiating results-oriented activities. In this chapter, you get to work on the details of your business start-up, which include:

- The mission statement
- Defining your product or service and its benefits
- Preparing your competitive analysis
- Defining the location and required improvements
- Identifying your equipment and inventory requirements
- Documenting your personnel requirements
- Listing the professionals involved in the business

Writing Your Mission Statement

Every business must have a mission. If it doesn't, the business will risk having a lack of focus and direction. Typically, a business initiative begins because a need has been identified in a specific industry—what is commonly referred to as an industry gap. For example, you might start an enterprise that provides custom sewing for disabled individuals because department store clothing doesn't meet their needs. Your business mission statement should describe how you'll address that industry gap and should also define your company's goals. Defining your objectives and stating your mission will provide a clear and focused approach to operating your enterprise.

In the following worksheet, complete the questions as they relate to your business mission.

IDENTIFYING YOUR BUSINESS MISSION

1. What industry have you identified (for example, health care, graphic design, forest products, risk management, insurance, and so on)?

2. Write an industry overview of 200 words or more describing key characteristics and trends in the industry.

3. Define the industry gap you have identified that your business will address. (For example, laser printer new toner cartridges were expensive for business offices to purchase. To address this problem, toner cartridge recycling became an emerging business opportunity.)

4. How will your business provide a solution to this industry gap and will your business solve all or some of the problem?

5. List three obtainable goals you'd like your business to achieve.

Now that you've thought about the reasons you plan to start your business, you're ready to incorporate the preceding information into your business mission statement. Consider the following example:

It will be the mission of Parrots at Play, Inc. to provide new owners of African parrots a safe and effective training program on the care, grooming, and housing of African parrots, as well as information on local regulatory requirements related to exotic bird ownership. It will be the goal of this organization to enhance the owner's enjoyment of the bird and to ensure successful cohabitation, while increasing compliance with local laws.

In the Parrots at Play mission statement, the entrepreneur has identified specific retailer and customer needs the business will fulfill. They are as follows:

- First, pet store retailers have been selling exotic birds to inexperienced owners who have ended up returning the parrots because of a lack of understanding of how to supply proper care. Consequently, the ownership success rate is low and the retailer has difficulty selling the pet.
- Second, local governments have special handling laws on the books related to ownership of exotic animals. These regulations were being ignored often because pet owners were not aware of their existence. Compliance within the community is necessary. Compromising on enforcement could create an important community safety concern. Parrots at Play offers a solution to this industry gap.
- Third, the purpose of owning any pet is to experience enjoyment and companionship. If neither need is being met, pet sales will decline and pet stores could go out of business. The enjoyment factor is an important one in the pet industry.

As you can see, the industry gaps defined by Parrots at Play was the lack of proper training for the owners of African parrots on how to care for the parrots, meet regulatory requirements, and enhance the joy of ownership. By addressing these industry gaps, the company can generate income from the sale of ongoing training classes, how-to books for the owners, and fee-based one-on-one consultations at the owner's home. The products and services fill the gaps and create a solution. Now that I've demonstrated how a mission statement can be written, try to write yours in the following worksheet.

MISSION STATEMENT

Remember that your business mission statement will grow and change as the business grows and changes. Revisit your mission statement at least once per year to see if it still applies to your company's goals. As the business progresses, it will be your responsibility to direct your company's activities as defined by the mission statement. Staying on track will be your primary challenge as well as a determinant of future success.

Looking at Your Products and Services

Next, you want to flesh out and describe the products or services you plan to offer consumers. In a world full of choices, maintaining a product focus can be a difficult management exercise. Changing trends, new customer demands, and fast-running fads threaten a business's ability to remain defined. Consider the recent changes in the offerings of gasoline/service stations. For years, when you pulled up to a filling station, your options were to purchase one of three types of gasoline: regular, unleaded, or premium. The other products or services available at gas stations were auto related, such as auto repair, tires, and compressed air. Today, however, gasoline as a product is partner to a myriad of other choices. You can fill up your car with gas, buy a hot dog, grab a newspaper, treat yourself to coffee and breakfast, buy a lottery ticket, obtain a prepaid telephone card, and in some cases, even buy cards and flowers. Changing trends in the commuting work force created a shift in the function of gasoline stations. So, too, will your business need to keep up to date with trends in your chosen industry and provide products and services to meet new demands. Maintaining a clear definition of your product or service is integral to meeting the needs of your customers.

The following are examples of products and services defined by industry. Look them over and then define your own products and services.

- Hair salon: Hair cutting/styling, hair-care products, manicures, facial waxing, image consulting.
- Doggie day care center: Daytime dog socialization, dog grooming, dog-care products,
dog food, and dog treats.
- Greeting card recycling manufacturer: Recycle paper into handmade paper greeting cards, invitations, and stationary.
- Nurse practitioner in private practice: Sports, travel, and college physicals; immunization clinics; workplace training; contracted services to physicians.
- Car wash: Self-service auto spray washers, auto detailing, car-cleaning products from vending machines, and full-service automatic car wash.

Now it's your turn to define your product or service in the following worksheet.

DEFINING YOUR PRODUCT OR SERVICE

1. Name your type of business: ____________________

2. Define your products and/or services:

____

____

____

____

____

____

Next you want to define the benefits of your product to the customer. Benefits are important to understand, as they will form the basis of customers' reasons for purchasing your product or service. The trick is to understand what discomfort the customer is experiencing. If your customer is burned out from overwork and you're a travel agent, for example, you could provide the benefit of hassle-free planning and delivery of a dream vacation. No stress! No inconvenience! No bother! Just a service that cures the pain. The business makes the sale and the customer makes the trip to paradise.

In looking at another example, assume you decide to open a graphic design studio. Customers will need your services for logo development, layout and design, newsletter production, and so on. Key benefits to your customers might include the following:

- Proficiency in PC and Mac applications
- Flexible production schedules to meet customers' last-minute needs
- Competitive pricing
- One thousand industry-related connections to printers, mail-order services, artists and illustrators, mailing-list providers

Articulating the benefits or value-added characteristics of your product or service allows the customer to judge the actual value associated with your offerings. Successful businesses cash in on this concept consistently, so using the following worksheet, clearly define your benefits to your customers.

CUSTOMER BENEFITS

DESCRIPTION OF THE PRODUCT:	BENEFIT TO CUSTOMERS:

When customers aren't happy with your business, they usually won't complain to you. Instead, they'll complain to just about everyone they know and take their business to the competition next time. That's why an increasing number of businesses are making follow-up calls or mailing satisfaction questionnaires after the sale is made. They find that if they promptly follow up and resolve a customer's complaint, the customer may be even more likely to do business than a customer who didn't have a complaint!

In many business situations, the customer will have many more interactions after the sale with technical, service, or customer support people than they did with the salespeople. So if you're serious about retaining and getting referrals, these interactions are the ones that matter. Handle them with the same attention and focus that you handle sales calls.

Looking at Your Competition

Your competitors will be keeping track of what you're providing to the customer so they can effectively compete against you. Staying abreast of what the competition is doing enhances a business's ability to respond in the market place. A competitive analysis needs to be completed as a critical step to your start-up. Identifying the competition within your geographic location will help you pinpoint appropriate advertising strategies and the best use of your defined benefits to the customer. Because you've completed the customer benefits analysis, you should be able to prepare a competitive analysis. In doing so, remember that competitors may be discovered in unlikely places.

For example, automobile dealerships have a new, indirect competitor found through the increased use of the Internet. Not so long ago, consumers seldom shopped for new and used cars online. Today, those looking to buy a car commonly utilize the Internet to obtain information on comparative pricing, availability, variety of offerings, and delivery options.

Dealerships have been required to learn how to respond to this growing consumer trend. Your competitive analysis will need to be thorough in determining all of the possible challengers to your business.

Sources for identifying the competition are found in all sorts of places. Start with the telephone book Yellow Pages and target those businesses that are within a five-mile radius of your proposed location. Then move on to my top ten list of methods for identifying your competition.

- Search the Internet.
- Visit professional clubs to seek out networking opportunities and collect business cards.
- Contact metropolitan and local chambers of commerce for a directory listing.
- Visit a few retail printing shops because they often display bulletin boards featuring a variety of business cards for review.
- Contact industry trade associations for a listing of members in your geographic area. Additionally, talk with distributors from the industry, because they are a great source of information.
- Hit the pavement and visit the competitor's location as a customer.
- Read print media like newspapers and magazines for current ads. Clip them out and put them in your five-subject notebook.
- Talk to your neighbors and family members. What they know could save you in time and oversight.
- Listen to different radio stations. Take detailed notes describing the competition's broadcasted offerings.
- Ask a competitor about the competition. As crazy as this sounds, an established business owner will know all the players in the arena. Listen closely if he or she is willing to share information.

One of the most common suggestions you'll get on how to compete against big national competitors is to emphasize service. If you understand service to mean that you smile at every customer and say, "hello," you probably won't be able to compete—or even survive. But if you understand service to mean providing additional services, you're still in the ballgame. Some hardware stores, for example, faced with a new Wal-Mart across the street, survive by offering services like lawn mower repair, skate sharpening, and key duplicating.

Complete one competitive analysis sheet for each competitor you've identified, using the following worksheet.

COMPETITIVE ANALYSIS WORKSHEET

Competitor's name: ____________________

Location/address: ____________________

Mailing address: ____________________

Telephone number: ____________________

Fax number: ____________________

E-mail address: ____________________

Web site: ____________________

Owner's name: ____________________

Number of years in business: ____________________

Number of employees: ____________________

Hours of operation: ____________________

How does the customer benefit from buying their product or service?

____

____

What color scheme is presented in their marketing materials?

____

What kind of promotional items do they use to sell their product or service?

____

____

How does the customer currently obtain their product or service?
(Describe the channels of distribution.)

____

____

Identify pricing strategies:

What are the terms of sale?

What is accepted tender: cash, credit/debit cards, personal checks, travelers' checks, money orders?

What is their major target market? Who do they primarily sell to?

What is their percentage of market share?

The main strengths of this competitor are:

Identified weaknesses are:

Additional notes and comments:

You'll want to scrutinize those businesses that pose the biggest threat to your business's targeted percentage of market share. In the final analysis, if the results of the competitive analysis identifies too many competitors in your local area, you may want to research another type of business. Remember that the objective is to fulfill a need where there is a consumer demand for a product or service. If the competitive analysis says, "don't go there," don't go there. Find another need and create a new business concept.

> One of the most important traits for business success is being cheap! In almost any business, if your cost structure is just a couple of percentage points lower than your competitors', you can have a huge competitive advantage.
>
> Also, as you hire people, you have a challenge getting them to adopt the same frugal mindset that you acquired by skimping during the early days of your business.

Location, Location, Location

We've all heard the phrase, "location, location, location." Location is a critical factor in pulling customers to your business, especially for retail. "Gray flannel" professionals like lawyers, accountants, insurance brokers, and stockbrokers seek out locations that will provide access to financial markets, business customers, infrastructure, easy parking, and cutting-edge technology and utilities. Their business depends on it. For you, it could mean being located on the side of the street where traffic can get in and out most easily. Ease in getting to your site may impact your customer flow and volume. Be sure to prepare a location analysis before signing a lease, constructing a building, or making any final decision about your location.

Study traffic flow and record the high and low traffic periods. Sit in the parking lot, on the side of the road, or near the proposed location to study the traffic. Count the number of vehicles that travel in and out of the location. If at all possible, try categorizing the type of vehicles that you see. For example, if you see a minivan, it may suggest the driver is an individual with a family. Visit the same site at different times of the week and day. The objective is to capture enough traffic data to support consumer traffic assumptions.

Analyzing and planning for the geographic location of your business also includes planning the potential use of internal space. Drawing out the utilization of space will help you to determine whether the space is appropriate. Even if your business will be operated as a home-based business, this step is essential. Easy-to-use interior design computer software is available for this task at your local computer store.

Use the following worksheet to scope out the possibilities.

LOCATION ANALYSIS FORM

1. Proposed location address: ____________________

2. Town/city of/zip: ____________________

3. Define the closest intersection: ____________________

4. List the other types of businesses around your location:

____

____

____

____

____

5. Number of square feet available for your business: ____________________

6. Cost per square foot: ____________________

7. Utilities included? ❑ Yes ❑ No

8. Maintenance included? ❑ Yes ❑ No

9. Windows in the front? ❑ Yes ❑ No

10. Number of driveways into the location: ____________________

11. Number of traffic lights near the location: ____________________

12. Are there hills, hard to find driveways, or blind corners to the property?
    ❑ Yes ❑ No

OPERATIONAL DESCRIPTION AND ANALYSIS OF YOUR OPERATIONAL FACILITY

1. Location Address: ______________________________

____

2. Total square footage: ______________
   Administrative: ______________
   Production: ______________
   Warehouse: ______________
   Other: ______________

3. Describe how the facility will be used:

____

____

____

4. Is there space/land available for expansion if needed? ❑ Yes ❑ No
   If yes, describe. If no, how will additional space/facility needs be handled?

____

____

____

5. Is there a skilled pool of potential employees available close by? ❑ Yes ❑ No

6. Is the facility accessible via public transportation? ❑ Yes ❑ No

7. Is the facility easily accessible for delivery and service vehicles? ❑ Yes ❑ No

8. Does the facility feature loading docks or bays? ❑ Yes ❑ No

9. What geographic area is served from this facility?

____

10. Is there adequate employee parking? ❑ Yes ❑ No

11. Is there adequate customer parking? ❑ Yes ❑ No

12. Is the facility leased or owned? ❑ Leased ❑ Owned
    Monthly lease/mortgage payment: ____________

    Length of lease or mortgage: ____________

    Terms of lease: ____

    ____

    Are there any restrictions contained in your lease? ❑ Yes ❑ No
    If so, what are they?

    ____

13. What is the zoning classification of the property? ____________

    Does the classification prohibit any business activities? ❑ Yes ❑ No
    Explain: ____

    ____

    ____

14. Average monthly utility costs:
    Electricity: ____________

    Gas: ____________

    Water/sewer: ____________

15. Average monthly maintenance costs: ____________

16. Average monthly cost for outside services: ____________

17. Annual real estate tax liability: ____________

In addition, to determine whether potential locations will fit with your product or service needs, complete the following four worksheets, which help you pin down exactly how you will operate your business by asking you to fully describe your production or service processes; your order-fulfillment and distribution processes; your quality assurance and control processes; and your insurance, legal, and regulatory issues. These worksheets may take some time to complete, but by fully understanding the processes you intend to put into place and the issues you may have to work through, you stand the best chance of finding the perfect location for your new business.

PRODUCTION/SERVICE PROCESSES

1. Provide a brief description of your production/service processes.

____

____

____

____

____

2. Describe how each of the following is incorporated within your process design.

Operational flexibility: ______________________________

____

Worker safety: ______________________________

____

Coordination of tasks: ______________________________

____

Equipment accessibility: ______________________________

____

Space utilization: ______________________________

____

Raw materials storage: ______________________________

____

Materials movement: ______________________________

____

Materials handling/storage: ______________________________

____

Quality control/assurance: ______________________________

3. What advantages/strengths do your production/service processes exhibit?

---

4. What disadvantages/weaknesses are manifest in your production/service processes?

---

5. Will you contract with any outside vendors to provide product components or services that will be part of your final offering? ❑ Yes ❑ No
   If yes, discuss who these subcontractors and/or suppliers are likely to be.

---

6. Justify your make/buy decision rationale in terms of cost savings, capabilities, inventory financing, labor availability, or other pertinent factors.

---

7. List, in detail, the specific costs associated with these outside products and services.

---

8. List all other costs associated with the production/service process.

Is any portion of your production process proprietary? ❑ Yes ❑ No
If yes, does a patent protect the process? ❑ Yes ❑ No

ORDER FULFILLMENT AND DISTRIBUTION

1. Describe the process by which customers' orders are taken, processed, and delivered.

2. Who will be responsible for order processing?

3. How will orders be communicated/transmitted from the salesperson to the order-fulfillment department?

4. What will be the average time from an order being placed to it's being shipped?

5. What processes will ensure orders are filled accurately and on a timely basis?

6. Identify your primary (1) and secondary (2) distribution channels:
   - ❑ Direct to consumer: Internet, retail, catalog, telemarketing sales force
   - ❑ Direct to business: Internet, catalog, telemarketing, sales force
   - ❑ To distributors for resale
   - ❑ To retailers
   - ❑ To manufacturers: For added value or for use in their product

7. How will your products reach your customer?
   - ❑ Own fleet
   - ❑ Common carrier
   - ❑ Express shipper
   - ❑ U.S. Postal Service
   - ❑ Other

8. Will private shippers transport on short notice? ❑ Yes ❑ No

9. Will there be additional charges to you? ❑ Yes ❑ No

10. How will shipments be made/charged?
    - ❑ F.O.B. origination
    - ❑ F.O.B. destination
    - ❑ C.O.D.
    - ❑ Other

11. What is the average shipping cost per order or unit? ____________________

E-mail, intranets, faxes, and voice mail are fine for accelerating the transfer of factual information. But when your communication involves any emotion—such as expressing different options—a face-to-face meeting is by far the best bet, with a traditional, interactive phone conversation a distant choice.

Why is face-to-face communication so important? As we get more efficient at communicating facts electronically, we tend to forget how much emotion we convey through body language and voice tone. For example, when I tell someone with words that I disagree, my tone, posture, smile, and eye contact says, "I value and respect your opinion and enjoy working with you . . . even through I disagree with you on this point."

QUALITY ASSURANCE AND CONTROL

1. Describe the controls in place to ensure quality throughout the production/service process.

2. How will you monitor the quality of your finished product?

3. Will purchased raw materials, components, or supplies be inspected upon arrival?
   ❑ Yes ❑ No Describe the process.

4. Will the company seek to obtain any quality certifications?
   ❑ Yes ❑ No If yes, explain.

5. How will quality issues be conveyed to employees?

6. What systems will be put in place to solicit customer feedback regarding quality issues?

INSURANCE, LEGAL, AND REGULATORY ISSUES

1. What types of insurance and coverage amounts will be needed for your business?

2. What type of ongoing legal advice and assistance will your company need?

3. What licenses and permits are required by law?

4. What regulations apply to your business?

5. Will employees need training in regulatory compliance? ❑ Yes ❑ No

6. What environmental regulations apply to your business?

7. Does your business require zoning permits, health permits, or environmental approvals to begin/continue operation? ❑ Yes ❑ No

8. Note any pending regulatory changes that could positively or negatively affect the nature and timing of your opportunity.

Identifying Supplies, Equipment, and Inventory Needs

Every business needs some type of equipment, supplies, or inventory.

- Equipment is usually an asset that you keep and maintain, such as a computer, forklift, or copier.
- Inventory refers to those items purchased for resale. If you're an automobile dealer, for example, the cars you purchase from the manufacturer for resale to the customer are your inventory.
- Supplies are generally described as items used to operate the business, such as staplers and staples, copier paper, and the fuel for the forklift.

Identifying those specific needs will help you plan in advance for the purchases. Use the following forms to assist you with locating and pricing supplies and equipment and to determine how you will process your inventory.

SUPPLIES ACQUISITION LIST

Description/ Number	Supplier Information	Cost	Quantity	Discount	Lead Time

After you've completed your list of supplies, consider issuing purchase orders for the items you've identified. This will allow you to easily track the order and delivery of each item. Your local office supply store will carry prenumbered purchase order forms in a generic format you can use for this purpose.

EQUIPMENT

1. List the production and operations equipment you currently own.

Description	Purchase Date	Cost	Purpose/Need

2. List your planned production and operations equipment purchases.

Description	New or Used?	Planned Date	Cost	Purpose/Need

3. List the office and administrative equipment you currently own.

Description	Purchase Date	Cost	Purpose/Need

4. List your planned office and administrative equipment purchases.

Description	New or Used?	Planned Date	Cost	Purpose/Need

5. List the vehicles you currently own.

Description	Purchase Date	Cost	Purpose/Need

6. List your planned vehicle purchases.

Description	New or Used?	Planned Date	Cost	Purpose/Need

7. Describe any processes in place to guide equipment purchases.

8. Have you examined leasing as a means of equipment acquisition?
   ❑ Yes ❑ No

9. Do you currently lease any equipment? List and identify lease terms.

10. Do you plan to make use of short-term equipment rentals? ❑ Yes ❑ No
    What types of equipment do you anticipate renting and under what circumstances?

11. How will you monitor equipment maintenance?

12. How will equipment replacement decisions be made?

13. Describe the system you will utilize to maintain equipment records.

14. Have you identified and evaluated potential sources of equipment rentals?
    Summarize your findings.

INVENTORY MANAGEMENT

1. Briefly describe your inventory control procedures. Be sure to include information about average inventory levels, order cycles, inventory shrinkage control, and anticipated inventory turnover rates.

2. Who will be responsible for inventory control?

3. How often will a physical inventory count be conducted?

4. Who will be responsible for counting?

5. Will you use production schedules incorporating material and inventory records?
❑ Yes ❑ No

6. Will any outside inventory warehousing be necessary? ❑ Yes ❑ No
If so, how will these needs be determined?

7. What will be the minimum level of inventory you will maintain?

8. By supplier, list and describe the order process and normal lead time(s).

9. What will be the minimum amount of time necessary to completely produce your products/services?

10. If you will be selling a product, what will be the normal time for goods in distribution?

11. Describe the process by which sales information will be communicated to production and purchasing.

12. Describe your inventory forecasting methods (for example, sales history, set minimum/maximum, computer models).

Personnel Requirements

Personnel requirements are a part of every business enterprise, even if you're the sole proprietor doing everything yourself. Operational tasks demand ownership. Someone must take responsibility for completing daily operational activities, or you'll lose track of the business, resulting in a loss of the business itself. If you, as the owner, cannot complete all the tasks required, you'll need to hire someone to do the work.

> If you're starting a small business, you may think, "I don't need employment policies—that's the kind of bureaucratic nonsense that I'll leave to the big corporations." Well, that's what I thought when I went into business, but I soon found that a few basic policies help avoid arguments and misunderstandings and decrease your chances of losing lawsuits.
>
> When you have more than a dozen employees, I'd recommend you create an employee handbook that lays out in clear, simple language what is and isn't acceptable in the workplace and that outlines grievance procedures.
>
> But don't throw together an employee handbook yourself unless you're willing to spend the money to hire an attorney who specializes in employment to review it.
>
> Company handbooks have been seen by the courts as legally binding contracts, and employees have successfully sued companies for not honoring their own handbooks.

The following worksheet will help you get a handle on your general workforce requirements.

PRODUCTION WORKFORCE

1. Total number of employees needed: ____________________

   Total permanent employees: Full time: ____________________

   Part time: ____________________

   Total temporary/contract employees Full time: ____________________

   Part time: ____________________

2. Will you use temporary labor? ❑ Yes ❑ No
   If yes, under what circumstances?

3. Who will be responsible for the decision to utilize temporary workers?

4. What are your anticipated product/service hours?

5. What skills and qualifications must employees possess?

6. Do any employees require specialized certifications? ❑ Yes ❑ No
   Explain.

7. Who will directly supervise production/service employees?

8. Will the business operate more than one production shift? ❑ Yes ❑ No

9. For each product or service, describe the number of worker hours required to produce a unit.

10. What types of production records will be required?

11. How and with what frequency will production requirements/service schedules be communicated?

12. Who will be responsible for monitoring productivity?

PERSONNEL REQUIREMENT FORM

1. Date prepared: ______________________________

2. Job title: ______________________________

3. The objective of this position is to:

____

4. Job description and duties:

____

____

____

____

____

____

5. Basic qualifications required:

____

____

____

____

6. Position requires:

❑ Full time ❑ Part time ❑ Outsourced resources

7. Projected wage per hour: ______________________________

8. Required number of hours per week or outsourced contract budget amount:

____

9. Hire the position on or before: ______________________________

To build a winning team, you not only need to show people what direction the company is headed in, but you need to get them to "buy into" this direction. Otherwise, you can't expect people to support a group if they don't agree with where it's headed—or worse, don't even know where it's headed.

Keeping Records

Financial accountability in your business activities serves two purposes. First, it provides you with the dollars and cents data you need to monitor your business and help you make appropriate management decisions. Second, it imposes controls within your organization to create operational checks and balances. Without financial accountability, you, as a business owner, will never understand the true status of the enterprise.

Creating a record-keeping system for your business will likely require the help of a professional like an accountant, a fee-based service provider. If you're not prepared to spend money on an accountant, check out the options for free and confidential advice available in your area. The first place to call is your local Small Business Development Center, where you can set up an appointment with a business adviser who will help you develop an initial record-keeping system. To find your closest SBDC logon to *www.asbdc-us.org*. Refer to the resource directory provided in this workbook for other advisory services.

Your financial record-keeping system should keep track of the following:

- Cash receipts
- Cash disbursements
- Inventory
- Daily cash flow monitoring

Depending on the size and type of business you have, other areas may need to be tracked, like work-in-progress, accounts receivable, and accounts payable. Seek professional, one-on-one advice for handling your specific needs.

To get you started with the basics, prepare two separate journals: one for cash receipts and the other for cash disbursements.

Cash Receipts Journal

Using a green ledger pad or an electronic spreadsheet, begin the cash receipts journal with the following information:

- **Type of journal:** Cash receipts journal
- **Business name:** Enter your business name.
- **Accounting period:** Note the period of time representing the transactions recorded; for example, April 1, 2002 to March 31, 2003.

Next, set up the columns of the worksheet to read as follows:

- **Transaction date:**
- **Received from:** List the company or individual
- **Tender:** How did you get paid?
- **Check or money order number:**
- **Amount received:**
- **Received for:** Describe why you received the money; for example, daily retail sales, payment of invoice #1234, refund of utility deposit.

It is very important to describe why the money was received so that the year-end reconciliations for taxes accurately reflect the sources of cash received. Receipt of a utility refund, for example, is a return of cash from prepaid deposits and not income from sales. Keeping the record straight could alter tax liability.

Cash Disbursement Journal

Cash disbursement journals are used to help you keep track of the money you disburse (or spend) out of the business. The cash disbursement journal is set up in a pattern similar to that of a cash receipts journal but with more definition as to the allocation of how the money was spent. You begin with the same heading format.

- **Type of journal:** Cash disbursements journal
- **Business name:** Enter your business name.
- **Accounting period:** Note the period of time representing the transactions recorded; for example, April 1, 2002 to March 31, 2003.

The following headings should be placed in each column:

- **Transaction date:**
- **Paid to:** Name of business or individual
- **Tender:** How did you make the payment? Check? Cash?
- **Check number:**
- **Amount paid:**

After these headings have been entered, place the headings for your expenses across the top of the page. You might use the following headings:

- Advertising
- Inventory
- Rent
- Gas

- Office supplies
- Vehicle maintenance
- Postage
- Owner's draw

Automating Your Records

Eventually, you may decide to delegate your record-keeping system to a computer system. In today's market there are a myriad of accounting software options available to you as a small business owner. The key is to work with a certified financial professional to discover the best system for your business. Be sure to do the following:

- Ask other business owners about the types of software they use.
- Investigate the options with sales representatives.
- Refer to Web sites that allow you to download a sample of the software to try. Popular options include Peachtree accounting, AccountMate, and Quick Books Pro. You may want to create a list of options and criteria in your five-subject notebook to help you evaluate the various offerings.
- Set a budget for the purchase of the software, for its installation, and, most important, for training.
- Prepare a record-keeping fallback plan in the event you experience a short-term problem when converting records to an automated system.
- Seek out reliable and proficient outsourced users of the accounting software who could provide mentoring, drop-in services, and rescue!
- Keep an open mind. If the software isn't a fit for you or your business, get rid of it and begin again. It is far better to have a system that is easy to use and understand than to have one with all the bells and whistles that only serve to confuse.
- Remember that automated systems need to offer comprehensive data that will lead to an understanding of the financial picture and will assist the entrepreneur in the decision-making process.

The Professionals of Record

The term "professionals of record" refers to the members of your management team who will work with you as you build your enterprise. It doesn't matter whether these professionals are hired, outsourced, family, friends, or community members. What does matter is that you establish this team well in advance of opening your business. This B.A.I.L. team will serve as your sounding board, mentor, advocate, and service provider. The B.A.I.L. team consists of:

- Banker
- Accountant
- Insurance Agent
- Lawyer

In addition to these professionals, you may want to include a financial management service, business advisers, an industry specialist–and maybe a really good fortune teller. The point is to surround yourself with knowledgeable individuals who, in a crisis or a pinch, could professionally assist you with their problem-solving skills. Securing these individuals' support before you open ensures that an established crisis management team is in place before a management crisis hits. It also allows you to establish a relationship with professionals who will provide you with services that promote your business's safety, security, and success.

The following is a checklist of the activities you should have completed through this section of the workbook.

BUSINESS PLANNING CHECKLIST

Have you . . .

- ❑ Defined your business concept?
- ❑ Defined the industry and written an industry overview?
- ❑ Identified an industry gap?
- ❑ Created an innovative solution to the industry gap?
- ❑ Written your mission statement?
- ❑ Defined your product or service?
- ❑ Described the benefits to your customers?
- ❑ Prepared the competitive analysis?
- ❑ Identified possible locations?
- ❑ Prepared a location analysis?
- ❑ Developed potential floor plans?
- ❑ Written directions to the potential locations?
- ❑ Prepared equipment and inventory requirements?
- ❑ Prepared an acquisitions list?
- ❑ Established personnel requirements?
- ❑ Written job descriptions?
- ❑ Prepared a record keeping system?
- ❑ Developed your list of professionals of record?

Steps to Marketing Your Business

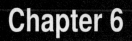

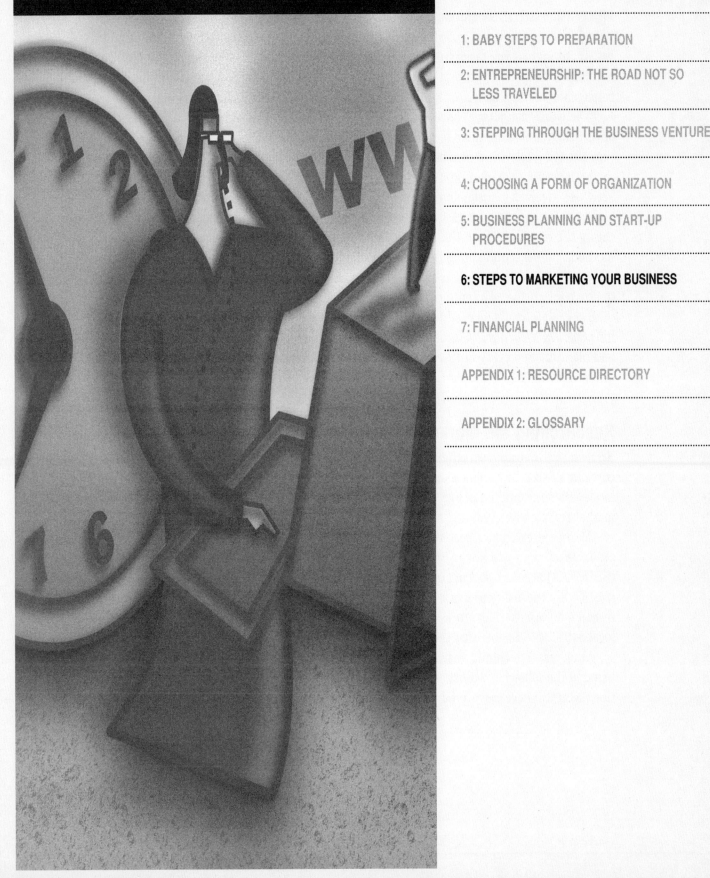

Chapter 6

Businesses are operational when customers purchase products or services from them. If there are no customers, there is no business. Pretty simple! Not so simple, though, is the task of pulling customers into a business and generating a sale. To accomplish the goal of generating customers and sales, business owners must embrace the concepts of marketing, better known as the marketing communications process.

The word "marketing" usually stirs up thoughts and images of newspaper or magazine advertising, junk mail, radio announcements, and unwanted faxes and e-mail, not to mention annoying television commercials. These commonly known advertising methods aren't really the same as marketing, however. The term "marketing" encompasses a variety of activities involved in a simple process. Collectively, they include researching the targeted customer base, creating a customer profile, developing a mix of advertising channels, educating the customer about the product or service, generating effective communication methods, and executing an ongoing advertising pull that builds customer loyalty and keeps the company positioned in front of the customer. In today's marketplace, businesses need to strive for customer retention and business loyalty. Developing a marketing and communications plan that is focused from the "customer, back," as articulated by Harry S. Dent in his book *The Roaring 2000s*, is essential to the success of the business. Competition is stiff and plentiful, and every business needs to prepare a solid marketing communications program that will ensure the generation of customers and sales.

Researching the Market

Knowing your customer is the first step to creating an effective marketing plan. Consumers come in all sizes and shapes, and your job is to identify those consumers who will spend money on your product or service. Finding a cluster of these consumers begins with the market research process.

Market research may become a challenging process. Therefore, employ all the resources available to help you, like the Small Business Development Center Information Clearinghouse (SBDCNET) at *http://sbdcnet.utsa.edu*. Also, your local Small Business Development Center (SBDC) has the ability to request market research from SBDCNET, where a staff of marketing research librarians will go to work on your questions, absolutely free, if you're a client of a local SBDC. (Remember that the SBDC offers free and confidential business counseling.)

Your research should answer at least twenty basic questions about your customer, listed in the following worksheet. By the time you've finished addressing these basic questions, you will have discovered what segment of the market you should target.

UNDERSTANDING YOUR CUSTOMER

1. What is the age group of your customers? ____________________

2. What is their stage of life (newly married, retired, married with college-bound teenagers, single)? ____________________

3. What gender are the majority of your customers? ❑ Male ❑ Female

4. What is the breakdown (percentage) of males and females? ____________________

5. What is the annual household income? ____________________

6. By percentage, how much of that income will customers spend on your product or service? ____________________

7. Describe the occupations of your customers (lawyers, mechanics, teachers, homemakers, and so on)? ____________________

____

8. Do your customers belong to a religious group? ❑ Yes ❑ No

   If so, in what religious practices and in what percentages?

____

____

____

9. What are your customers' ethnicities? ____________________

____

____

____

10. How much education have your customers completed?

    Breakdown by percentage: ______________

    High school and below: ______________

    Graduated from high school: ______________

    Some college completed: ______________

    Graduated with a two-year degree: ______________

    Graduated with a four-year degree: ______________

    Beyond four years of college completed: ______________

11. Where do your customers reside?

    Countries: ______________

    States: ______________

    Local geographic areas: ______________

12. What is the population of the area your business will serve?

13. What percentage of your targeted customer base has a computer in the household? ______________

14. Which of the following do your customers have:

    - ❑ Cable television
    - ❑ Web TV
    - ❑ Cellular telephone
    - ❑ In-home fax machine
    - ❑ Electronic calendar
    - ❑ Laptop computers
    - ❑ Beeper

15. What types of hobbies do your customers participate in?

    ____

    ____

16. What types of sports do your customers like?

    ____

    ____

17. What types of music and art are preferred by your customers?

---

18. What types of publications do your customers read?

---

19. Do your customers listen to audio books, music CDs, or motivational tapes?
 ❑ Yes ❑ No

20. Are there any other special characteristics related to your targeted customer base (disabled, veteran, hearing impaired, sight-impaired, and so on)?

Steer clear of the following ten common (and costly) sales mistakes of business owners:

- Believing the myth that the world will beat down the door of whomever builds a better mousetrap.
- Believing the myth of the natural-born salesperson.
- Not trying to improve your own selling skills.
- Not viewing every customer inquiry as a sales prospect that should be carefully wooed and aggressively followed up on.
- Emphasizing your product features rather than your customers' needs.
- Not building a rapport with a customer before diving into your sales presentation.
- Not making lots and lots of cold calls to prospective clients.
- Not pressing your customers for more information after first hearing, "I'm not interested."
- Not aggressively following up on prospects who express some interest.
- Not setting up a highly lucrative bonus or commission structure for talented salespeople.

Profiling Your Customer

Answering the questions in the preceding worksheet should have provided you with a pretty solid picture, or profile, of your targeted market and the demographics related to your customer base.

The next step is to write the customer profile or the conclusive description of the customer. The following is an example of what I mean:

Customer Profile for Decorative Medical Scrubs

Decorative Medical Scrubs typically attract registered nurses and licensed practical nurses who work full time in maternity and pediatric hospital wards. As medical professionals, they earn between $27,250 and $65,000 per year and generally purchase their own medical apparel. Sixty-three percent of pediatric nurses and fifty-one percent of maternity nurses are married with at least two children. They read professional magazines, enjoy crafts, attend religious services regularly, and vacation on cruise lines. Twenty-one percent of nurses in this group have also been divorced at least once.

Although I fabricated the information in the profile, you can see how the quantity of information provides a snapshot of the customer. Using this data, I could develop a plan to advertise in nursing publications, church bulletins, or parenting magazines. The purpose of the profile is to help determine the method to be used for advertising, promoting, and distributing the medical scrubs.

You don't have to be in business for too long before you figure out how hard it is to get new customers! Ads that simply describe your service or product often produce disappointing results. That's because you need to do more than just attract customers—you need to steal them away from the competitor who is currently serving them!

Consider new-customer offers: one-time-per-customer specials that lure new clients into your fold. These offers may include special pricing, buy-two-get-one-free offers, free-gift-with-purchase offers, extended warranties, money-back guarantees.
In a service business, consider free estimates, free appraisals, free first consultation, or a free trail period.

Remember that even most lawyers offer a free first consultation.

Your task will be to use the answers to those twenty questions about your own customers to develop a conclusive and comprehensive customer profile. My suggestion is that you use your five-subject notebook to record data and write your customer profile.

The Eight-Point Marketing Plan

Now that you understand to whom you are selling, think about how you will sell your product or service and through which media. The best way to organize your ideas on how to sell to your customers is to develop a marketing plan.

In an effort to help you understand and write a marketing plan, I've created a format and checklist of activities for you to pursue. You can begin with the format for a marketing plan.

Objective

Determine the goals to be achieved. Goals may include a targeted number of new customers, a certain sales amount, or increased inquiries or Web site hits. The following is an example of a marketing objective:

The objective of this marketing plan is to serve as a written, step-by-step guide for the management team of Parrots at Play, Inc. The company's intention is to increase sales at a rate of 5 percent per month for the next four months by introducing private label Parrots at Play merchandise and increasing consumer awareness of the company's other products and services.

Targeted Markets

Based upon the results of the market research obtained, list the groups to which the business will direct its marketing communications. For Parrots at Play, the options may include current parrot owners, pet stores, pet associations, publishers of pet newsletters, zoos, and animal shelters.

You never know what's going to work in marketing, so don't be afraid of making lots of mistakes (as long as they're small mistakes!). With that in mind, however, keep the following in mind: Never spend lots of money on any marketing program until you see that it's bringing in money, never assume an ad agency or marketing expert can guarantee results, make small test promotions and put in that extra effort to carefully measure results, ask every customer how they heard about your business, and track the response to every promotional effort.

Certain marketing avenues will work for your business, but you have to find the right mix of media, ad copy, and ad design.

Identifying Trends

List key information on new trends in the industry as well as local trends that should be noted.

Referral and Channels of Support

Determine which organizations and other businesses may be interested in providing some kind of support for your objectives. For example, not-for-profit animal rights groups may be interested in helping to promote Parrots at Play merchandise in exchange for a per unit contribution during a fundraiser.

Competitive Challenges

Investigate the communications being delivered by the competition. Collect brochures, ads, and other such materials and note the messages being sent. Define what your approach will be and your unique selling proposition that will make your business more valuable in the marketplace.

Strategic Approach

Here you'll actually write out the activities you'll pursue to deliver your message, increase awareness, and, hopefully, pull customers to your business. For example, the Parrots at Play scenario may develop in this way.

- Provide free pet parrot seminars at the public library while wearing the new T-shirt and displaying other Parrots at Play merchandise.
- Create a picture of a parrot and have it distributed to schools, pet stores, and the humane association for use in a coloring contest. The winners will receive items from the new line of Parrots at Play merchandise.
- Approach the community newspaper editors about contributing an article on fascinating facts about parrots. This will create interest on the part of the customer and help increase name recognition.
- Contact the gift shop manager at the humane association and offer to contribute $2 from the sale of each T-shirt if the manager agrees to carry the line.
- Develop a four-color catalog of the merchandise and send it to all existing parrot owners from a purchased mailing list.
- Create a new display area in the Parrots at Play retail location to showcase the merchandise.

Activities Timeline

Make a calendar for each month there will be marketing and promotional activities, beginning with the first month of your marketing campaign. The time line should include the type of activity, the date of execution, the term of the activity (how long it will go on for), and an activity identification number.

Auditing Results

Define the method for tracking the outcome of your marketing and communications efforts. Be sure to ask each customer if he or she has seen the advertising or read the article. List a fictitious name in an ad so that when a customer calls and asks for John, you'll know he or she saw the ad in the local paper.

These techniques help you define the results of the marketing plan. If you don't track the results, you don't learn which activities worked and which ones failed. Auditing is critical to future planning and development of your marketing activities. More important, it impacts the amount of money you'll spend on each activity. If the audit reveals that the classified ads did not generate enough sales, for example, you may not be inclined to invest any more money into classifieds.

Putting It All Together

Using this eight-point marketing plan as an ongoing tool will help you develop a comprehensive, well-thought-out approach to marketing your business.

THE EIGHT-POINT MARKETING PLAN WORKSHEET

Objective: The objective of this marketing plan is to provide a written guide for:

List your targeted markets.

Identifiable trends include:

Referrals and channels of support are as follows:

Competitive challenges include:

COMPETITOR'S NAME	WHAT MESSAGE IS SENT	ACTION NEEDED

Your strategic approach is as follows:

Activity #1:

____

____

Activity #2:

____

____

Activity #3:

____

____

Activity #4:

____

____

Activity #5:

____

____

Activity #6:

____

____

Activity #7:

____

____

List events in your activities timeline:

Type of activity	Date	Term	ID Number

Define your method of auditing your results and list your outcomes.

A standard press kit consists of a personalized pitch letter, press release, company backgrounder (short history of your company), business card, photos or slides of product(s), testimonial sheet, data sheet, folder, and mailing envelope.

To conserve costs, consider using a mini press kit, which can be as effective as a full-blown press kit. It should include the following: a personalized pitch letter, press release, business card, and #10 business envelope.

Establishing a Marketing Budget

In addition to using your eight-point marketing plan, you need to establish a marketing budget. How much you spend, however, is unique to your business. Using the following worksheet along with a pencil and a good eraser, try a variety of allocations for your marketing dollars.

There are many compelling reasons to attending trade shows. Don't view them as just an opportunity to write orders. In fact, in many industries, few orders are taken on the trade show floor. Instead, consider the many reasons companies attend trade shows: to get new leads, to build relationships with customers, to launch new product lines, to seek distributors or sales representatives, to "pre-sell" to customers before sales visits, to check out the competition, to get industry media coverage, to attend seminars, and to network.

Preparing a marketing plan takes time and work. Always continue to gather information and think creatively while developing your business's marketing strategy. Watch television ads, read different publications, and explore unlikely sources (such as the back of a cereal box) for clues about what's happening in the world around you. Search for subtle trends in various industries and play with ideas on how those trends may impact your business. As you make these observations, begin to fill in the following worksheet, which helps you decide where to spend your advertising and promotion dollars.

Businesses ranging in size from major airlines to local car washes rely heavily on frequent-buyer programs for good reason: They work!

The most common approach is to give customers a card that's punched or recorded in the computer, resulting in a free or reduced-price product or service offering after a specified number of regular-price purchases. For example, ten haircuts may net one free one.

Another approach is to give regular customers a discount on every purchase upon presentation of their frequent-buyer card.

The real power of a frequent-buyer program isn't just retaining customers with a standardized discount program. The real power is that it gives you information about customers that tells you when and what they're buying—so you can target mailings or phone calls to specific customers. And it tells you when customers aren't buying, so you know when you need to lure them back.

MARKETING PROGRAM BUDGET WORKSHEET

Marketing Vehicle	Specifics	Frequency	Cost/Year
Business cards			
Brochures			
Sales/data sheets			
General newspaper			
Magazines			
Specialty magazines			
Newsletters			
Videos			
Internet/Web site			
Yellow Pages			
Directories			
Memberships			
Trade associations			
Radio			
Television–local			
Television–cable			
Direct mail			
Billboards/outdoor			
Telemarketing			
Civic organizations			
Total marketing budget			

ADVERTISING AND PROMOTION

1. Based on your marketing program and budget, identify the media alternatives that best reach your target market.

2. Rate these media based on cost to reach 1,000 target customers.

3. Explain why you believe your combination of media provides you with the best opportunity to reach your marketing objectives.

4. How do your company logo and brand names assist with communicating your product or service benefits to your target market?

5. Who will be responsible for directing your promotional program and advertising?

Planning Your Opening Day

Even if you're kicking off a home-based consulting business or a plant-watering service, stage a grand opening event that gathers a crowd. The key is to establish the date that you officially arrive on the "open for business" scene and to stir up conversation about what your business provides. Plan a backyard barbecue with friends and family. Think about doing an open house so that people can stop by and congratulate you on your first day of business.

MINI-EVENT PLANNER

Event objective: ____________________

Planned day and date of the event: ____________________

Describe what type of event it will be (theme): ____________________

____

____

During what hours will the event be held? ____________________

Where will the event take place? ____________________

Tasks:

- ❑ Prepare the guest list: This should be a comprehensive list of anyone who will be vested in your success (family, friends, former business associates, politicians, and economic development agency personnel you've met and/or worked with).
- ❑ Invitations: Select quality paper stock that will get noticed and provide a professional appearance. Use a professional printer or home computer if you can achieve a professional result.
- ❑ Food: Keep food simple and uncomplicated. The easier it is to eat the more comfortable your guests will be. Easy eating entices more conversations and networking.
- ❑ Give-away: Plan to provide a drawing for a valuable gift. Gift baskets with books, magazines, gadgets, and a gift certificate for your services work well.
- ❑ Thank-you notes: Remember to always send a thank you note after the event. Be sure to handwrite the note and be sincere. Your guests should receive their thank-you notes within one week of the event.
- ❑ Publicity: Try to get a reporter to cover the event or send a photo and an article to your local newspapers.

Completing a Marketing Plan Checklist

To conclude this marketing section, utilize the following checklist of ways to help you stay on track while writing your marketing plan.

- Visit the local library and chat with a librarian about the resources available for small business research. If you're an inexperienced Internet user, be sure to get a demonstration of any Internet capabilities the library may have available and to ask for help in using search engines. Create a list in your notebook of the publications available at the library and of the what information they contain.
- Contact the economic development agencies in your area–like the Small Business Development Centers–for help with your market research.
- Contact your metropolitan and local chamber of commerce for information on your industry.
- Prepare market research using the twenty customer profile questions, trade journals, trade associations, and all other information gathered.
- Develop a conclusive and comprehensive written, customer profile.
- Establish your company's marketing objectives.
- Determine your targeted customer base.
- Research and identify industry and demographic trends.
- Make note of compatible industries that will serve as a referral base and channels of support for your marketing effort. List each support area.
- Seek out the competitive challenges. Learn what the competition is doing. Collect ads and brochures.
- Create a strategic approach to the marketplace. Develop marketing activities that pull in customers and sell your product or service. (Remember, be creative.)
- Complete your monthly timeline of activities.
- Document your marketing plan and record the results.

Avoid the ten following common (and costly!) advertising errors of business owners:

- Not tracking results.
- Not continually testing new ad media, new ad copy, and new ad offers.
- Advertising evenly throughout the year instead of concentrating the effort for more impact.
- Not choosing the ad media that's most effective for the target market and product or service being offered.
- Not continuously emphasizing the business's unique selling proposition.
- Failing to create a distinctive and consistent look and feel for the advertising.
- Failing to develop exciting promotions or events to maximize advertising impact.
- Not promoting separately and aggressively to current and past customers.
- Listening to advertising salespeople.
- Emphasizing product features instead of benefits to the customer.

Financial Planning

Chapter 7

Profitability is a fundamental and required objective for anyone engaging in an entrepreneurial enterprise. Without profits, businesses wouldn't exist, business growth would not be possible, and private sector jobs would be extinct. The nation's economy depends on the talents of our entrepreneurs to produce profits and create a strong economic base.

Because profitability is so important to the success of a small business enterprise, it's critical that you examine the financial aspects of your business idea. Financial analysis and planning will determine the economic feasibility of your business concept. Stepping through some financial exercises will help you project the potential for profits and determine whether you should proceed with the business start-up. Often, during the planning stages of a new business, an entrepreneur will discover that, while the business concept is good, the revenues would be insufficient and would not meet the entrepreneur's financial needs. It would be foolish to proceed with a business idea that wouldn't create a return on investment for the owner or that can't generate the profits required to ensure business continuation and growth.

The process of projecting your earnings and expenses acts as the final step in planning your business start-up. The effort you put into this area of planning will directly affect your chances of success.

Too many people equate annual planning with budgeting. Worse, when they budget, they simply extrapolate last year's number into next year's plan, perhaps increasing by 5 percent here and 6 percent there.

Instead, even if you're running a one-person business, you want to get a few words, not just numbers, into your annual plan. You don't need a full-fledged 100-page business plan—in fact, a big, detailed plan may take the focus away from what matters. What matters is the few big things the company is striving to do better or different next year. The annual planning process should focus on these few, important changes.

Five Financial Documents

There are, at minimum, five specific financial documents you should create in order to accurately project your company's financial future. They include the following:

- A list of financial assumptions
- A thirty-six-month income and expense projection
- A thirty-six-month cash flow projection
- A break-even analysis
- An inception balance sheet

These documents provide the foundation for your financial picture and provide a projected view of the revenues to be generated. Additionally, these documents identify operational expenses, the company's projected financial position, and minimum performance requirements needed to meet existing fixed costs. Accuracy in preparing these financial projections is very important, so please plan to spend a fair amount of time working up these numbers.

Although a crystal ball can't give you the absolute answers to your financial projections, there are tools available to help you with the process. One such tool is the Risk Management Association (RMA) annual statement studies that provide industry data and norms. You can find this publication at your local library or visit their Web site at *www.rmahq.org*. Other tools include industry financial data provided by trade associations, chambers of commerce, townships, and county economic development agencies.

A well-prepared financial plan is key to the success of any new business. Aspiring entrepreneurs need to have detailed information about their business's potential for profitability. This data may also be needed to attract investors, bankers, or new partners. Realistic assumptions, well-calculated projections, and a complete financial picture help ensure the success and profitability of any enterprise.

Financial Assumptions

The financial analysis and planning process begins with applying the information you have obtained from your market research and creating a list of assumptions. The list of assumptions consists of a series of statements that are the foundation of your financial projections. For example, if you were opening a café, your assumptions might be identified as follows:

- The café will provide seating capacity for fifty-six patrons.
- The café will operate between 8:00 P.M. and 2:00 A.M. six days per week, Tuesday through Sunday, representing thirty-six hours of operations.
- The customer will spend an average $6 per visit.
- The café will serve an average of 140 customers per day.

The concept is to use the information obtained through market research (see Chapter 6) to create reasonable assumptions about anticipated business activity. With the assumptions created in this example, you could project that the café could produce revenues of $5,040 per week by calculating 140 customers × $6 per visit × six days per week.

Remember that the assumptions must have some basis in concrete evidence. A common mistake among new business owners is the creation of unrealistic projections based on overly optimistic assumptions. The best approach is to be conservative. If the financial projections prove positive with a conservative approach, you're likely to exceed those projections when you're in full operation. This is a much better scenario than overprojecting and failing to meet the financial expectation. You'll need to create a list of assumptions for your business idea in a notebook.

Income and Expense Projections

After the assumptions have been identified, you can put them to use. During this activity you'll be creating a spreadsheet of projected income and expense. If possible, use an electronic spreadsheet program and produce the projections on your computer. If you don't have a computer, purchase a twenty-five-column ledger pad and proceed the old-fashioned way, with your pencil and eraser.

To start, put the heading "Income and Expense Projections" at the top of the spreadsheet. Next, label the columns as follows:

- Column one: Description
- Column two: Start-up
- Column three: The month and year you anticipate starting your operation.
- Column four through fifteen: Subsequent months and years of operations.
- Column sixteen: Total

Prepare one spreadsheet for each twelve-month period.

Along the left-hand column under "Description," list the income and expense categories. Be sure to include room for totals. While each business idea will have its own unique categories, there are standard items for all businesses, such as sales, postage, office supplies, rent, and so on. When you've completed the spreadsheet, it should look like the following sample.

BUSINESS INCOME PROJECTION

BUSINESS NAME	FOR THE YEAR ENDED
INCOME	
Sales	
(less returns and allowances)	
Net sales	
Cost of goods sold	
Beginning inventory	
(plus purchases)	
(plus freight, etc.)	
(less returns and allowances)	
Cost of goods available	
(less ending inventory)	
Cost of goods sold	
Gross profit on sales	
EXPENSES	
Salaries	
Rent	
Utilities	
Supplies	
Depreciation	
Taxes and licenses	
Repairs and maintenance	
Miscellaneous expenses	
Total expenses	
NET INCOME FROM OPERATIONS	
Other income	
(less other expenses)	
NET PROFIT BEFORE TAXES	
Income tax	
NET PROFIT AFTER TAXES	

BUSINESS EXPENSE PROJECTION FOR ONE MONTH

Business Name **Date:**

Variable Expenses

Salary of owner (required living expenses as a minimum) ______________

Employee wages and salaries ______________

Professional fees (accounting, legal, etc.) ______________

Advertising ______________

Materials or inventory ______________

Supplies ______________

Telephone (long distance) ______________

Maintenance and repair ______________

Miscellaneous (petty cash, postage, shipping, etc.) ______________

Other (list) ______________

Total Variable Expenses ______________

Fixed Expenses

Rent for building ______________

Rent for equipment ______________

Utilities ______________

Telephone (monthly fee) ______________

Loan payments and interest ______________

Taxes and licenses ______________

Insurance (if annual, divide by twelve) ______________

Other ______________

Total Fixed Expenses ______________

Total Business Expenses per Month ______________

Paying taxes isn't fun, but it's more fun than going through an audit! While you may have to pay a variety of taxes from employment taxes to sales taxes, income taxes will be the largest burden on your profitable company. Plan accordingly and pay your taxes regardless of how difficult others bills are to pay.

When your cash crunch is looking particularly severe, and you can't pay all of your creditors, decide which ones to pay first. While every situation is different, the following list provides a priority for your payments:

- Payroll and sales taxes
- Income and other taxes
- Utilities
- Wages
- Key suppliers
- Creditors

Cash Flow Projections

The income and expense spreadsheet is useful in determining sales and expenses; however, this may not realistically demonstrate the timing of cash coming into the business versus when the cash needs to flow out of the business. A cash flow projection is needed to calculate this critical element.

Before you start a business, your thoughts about finances may focus on how much money you can make and how long you'll have to work before your business becomes profitable. As soon as you start your business, however, your financial focus will quickly shift to cash flow. Even if your business is highly profitable, you're probably going to have less cash available than you may ideally like. How well you manage cash is going to have a major impact on the success—and often even the very survival—of your business.

Cash flow projections are set up similarly to the income and expense spreadsheet. The difference is that the cash flow projections will have different descriptions. The descriptions in column one should be set up as follows:

- Beginning cash
- Cash proceeds from loans
- Cash receipts from sales
- Cash receipts from accounts receivable
- Cash from other sources
- Total cash available
- Cash disbursements
- Deposits
- Cash disbursement items

The format allows you to schedule and project how cash will flow into and out of the business. Businesses like a café or store operate on a cash basis, where sales and cash receipts are the same. Businesses like manufacturers, consultants, and distributors, however, issue invoices for products and services provided and often don't receive payments for thirty or more days after billing the customer. A consultant may have terms that read, "Ten percent upon contract signing, net thirty days for work-in-progress invoices, and balance due upon completion of the project." Under these terms, the consultant receives a small retainer up front, but the customer may take thirty days before sending the next check for the work in progress. It is a common practice, in fact, for consultants to wait up to sixty days before receiving an invoice payment. This could hinder the consultant's ability to pay his or her business expenses on time.

On the income and expense spreadsheet, the consultant's sales would be recognized even though the cash wouldn't have hit the bank. That's why cash flow projections are so important. A business owner really needs to determine the actual timing of cash received so cash disbursements planning may take place. Always remember that cash is the ruler in any business, and whoever has the gold is the ruler.

Planning the flow of cash for your business is critical to operations. Seek professional assistance if you need help with this calculation. The Small Business Development Centers are the absolute best place to obtain technical assistance. The U.S. Small Business Administration has an excellent publication entitled "Understanding and Controlling Cash Flow" (publication FM-4). The cost is about $3. Ordering information is included in the resource directory at the end of this book.

If you're like me, before you dream of going into a new business, you dream of big, fat profits. But after you're in business, you dream instead of positive cash flow.

Crucial in controlling cash is having a detailed cash-flow projection, updated at least every month. But don't just add up the numbers—manage the numbers. Often, by careful management, you can realize huge cash savings without changing the course of the business.

Break-Even Analysis

The next financial document you'll need to prepare is the break-even analysis. Here you'll determine the actual amount of fixed costs (costs that are constant such as rent, lease payments, and loan obligations) required by your business and the sales volume needed to meet financial obligations. These costs are not directly related to sales.

CASH FLOW PROJECTION

CASH FLOW PROJECTION	CHITTY CHAT CAFÉ		
PREPARED: SEPTEMBER 2003	SEP-03	OCT-03	NOV-03
Beginning Cash	15,000.00	72,004.00	92,027.00
Cash Proceeds from Loans	40,000.00	—	—
Cash from Sales	21,840.00	24,026.00	25,742.00
Cash from A/R	—		
Cash from Other Sources	—		
Total Cash Available	76,840.00	96,030.00	117,769.00
Cash Disbursements			
Advertising	1,200.00	360.00	275.00
Auto Expense	78.00	55.00	60.00
Business Services	50.00	50.00	50.00
Bank Charges	24.00	32.00	35.00
Delivery Expense	153.00	192.00	220.00
Insurance-Workers Comp.	654.00	654.00	654.00
Insurance-Disability	52.00	52.00	52.00
Insurance-Business Package	95.00	95.00	95.00
Interest from Loans Expense	142.00	142.00	140.00
Office Expense	120.00	95.00	111.00
Postage	63.00	75.00	59.00
Rent	450.00	450.00	450.00
Repairs	75.00	33.00	25.00
Selling Expense	230.00	220.00	195.00
Subscriptions	12.00	—	11.00
Supplies	86.00	126.00	133.00
Telephone	125.00	125.00	125.00
Trade Dues	—	—	85.00
Travel Expense	15.00	35.00	40.00
Wages	1,126.00	1,126.00	1,126.00
Payroll Tax	86.00	86.00	86.00
Total Cash Disbursements	4,836.00	4,003.00	4,027.00
Ending Cash Balance	72,004.00	92,027.00	113,742.00

Note that cash should increase each month for a positive cash flow.
1. The ending cash balance becomes the beginning balance for the following month.
2. This analysis shows the flow of cash.
3. Notice the cash balances are different from profit.

A low-cost structure is essential for being competitive, and low overhead is crucial to reducing costs. Overhead costs don't directly make your product or deliver your service, and they don't directly benefit your customer. Overhead is like government bureaucracy—it just grows and grows. And the more it grows, the harder it is to take it away.

Unfortunately, too many employees love overhead! They love nice desks, new computers, new buildings, and deep carpet. But all these trappings of success are just that—traps—and every overhead expense threatens the company and every employee who works there.

The following worksheet is intended to simplify the break-even analysis for you by having you list your fixed costs. Accountants, comptrollers, and business managers work with complicated and detailed formulas for determining a business's break-even point. In the following worksheet, you simply determine the dollar amount you need to cover your fixed costs.

FIXED COSTS

Monthly rent	$________
Monthly lease payments	$________
Bank loan payments	$________
Automobile payment	$________
Equipment lease payment	$________
Insurance premiums monthly	$________
Average telephone cost	$________
Average heat and lights cost	$________
Other fixed costs	$________
Other fixed costs	$________
Other fixed costs	$________
Total monthly fixed costs	$________

Divide the total monthly fixed costs by the average unit price of your product or service. For example, the café scenario given as an example in the "Financial Assumptions" section of this chapter determined that the customer would spend an average of $6 per person. If the total monthly fixed costs of the café were $900, 150 customers would need to be served at this unit price to cover the basic fixed costs. In other words, think about how many units you need to sell in order to keep the doors open and be able to pay your bills to maintain operations.

The break-even analysis is intended to help you plan for profitability, gauge the impact on the operation when changes occur, and figure out the best use of your sales dollars. The more you learn about the break-even analysis, the better you'll be at managing your business and calculating ways to be profitable.

Suppose your overall profit margin is 5 percent—not an uncommon level for many smaller firms. But if you can cut your costs by just 5 percent, you profit will double. On the other hand, to get the same increase by boosting sales, you would have to increase sales by 100 percent. Chances are, cutting costs just a little bit would be a lot easier.

To attack your costs, take a look at every single expense item, starting with the biggest items! Get competitive bids for every product and service you buy!

Remember that there is no such thing as fixed costs. Often, lease rates, mortgage rates, and utility rates can be negotiated downward, especially if the market has shifted.

Balance Sheet

The final financial document to be prepared is the inception balance sheet. This document provides a snapshot of your business's financial position on the day you begin operations. Consider it the starting line or your financial launching pad. At the end of your first year, you'll compare the inception balance sheet with your year-end balance sheet to measure the progress you've made. Preparing a personal balance sheet is a good idea too, because doing so maintains a clear picture of both your business and personal financial positions.

Completing the balance sheet requires a baseline of information. Remember that the balance sheet is a summary of your current financial position. The dollar amounts provided should be calculated as of a specific period ending date, such as November 30, 2002. Everything you enter onto the balance sheet should be the balance as of that date.

While completing the balance sheet continue to use the phrase, "as of this period ending date, my balance was such and such." For example, as of November 30, 2002, my checking account balance was $1,233.00. As of November 30, 2002, my total loan balance for my car was $6,300.00. The objective is to calculate the actual balance or value of each balance sheet line item. The calculation includes items of value that you own and items you owe.

Complete the following worksheet to create the inception balance sheet for your new business.

INCEPTION BALANCE SHEET

Date prepared: ____________

Assets

Cash on hand: $ ____________

Cash in checking account: $ ____________

Cash in savings account: $ ____________

Prepaid insurance: $ ____________

Inventory: $ ____________

Equipment: $ ____________

Vehicles: $ ____________

Land and building: $ ____________

Deposits: $ ____________

Furniture and fixtures: $ ____________

Other assets: $ ____________

Total assets: $ ____________

Liabilities: $ ____________

Vendor/trade payables: $ ____________

Bank loan principal balance: $ ____________

Vehicle loan balance: $ ____________

Other liabilities: $ ____________

Other liabilities: $ ____________

Total liabilities: $ ____________

Owner's equity (O/E): $ ____________

(Total assets = liabilities + owner's equity)

Total assets: $ ____________

Total liabilities + O/E: $ ____________

Obtaining Financing

Should you decide to obtain financing now or in the future, your personal credit report and business financial information and statements will be basic to the evaluation of your business as an investment opportunity and will need to represent your best estimates of your financial requirements.

Your Credit Report

During this exciting period of new beginnings, it's appropriate to give your personal credit a checkup. Do this by requesting your credit report and seriously reviewing what's being reported about you. Should your business grow quickly, you may need financing, and your credit report will impact decisions of potential lenders. By resolving personal financial issues now, in the early stages of your business, you may be able to avoid future problems.

To request your credit report, write a letter to the reporting agencies and include your full name, social security number, home address, telephone number, date of birth, and copies of a utility bill and your driver's license. Other forms of identification may be substituted with the permission of the credit-reporting agency. For information on obtaining your credit history, contact the following credit bureaus:

- Experian: 888-397-3742
- Trans Union: 316-636-6100
- Equifax: 770-612-3200

Take the time to review each item on your credit history and work toward correcting any errors. For help with the credit repair process, seek out publications on the topic, such as *The Credit Repair Kit* by John Ventura and *Credit Repair, 4th Edition*, by Robin Leonard.

Financial Information and Statements

Any commercial lending institution or potential investor will scrutinize your past and projected financial performance to ensure that your business concept is viable and that you represent an acceptable risk. For a start-up business, you will need to include the following:

- Projected income statements for three years
- Projected cash flow statements for three years, one year by month and two years by quarter
- Projected balance sheets for three years, including an inception balance sheet

It is very important that these numbers be realistic and achievable. Any informed reader, like a commercial lender or a savvy investor, analyzes financial statements regularly–they understand them and can detect flaws quickly and easily.

For all of the projected (also referred to as pro forma) financial statements, be sure to discuss fully the assumptions you've made to develop the numbers. The statements themselves are almost meaningless unless they include an explanation that tells the reader how you arrived at your key financial projections. This section does not have to be long and elaborate. Simple and straightforward details will be sufficient. Whenever possible, provide documentation that lends credence to your assumptions. An example of this would be a situation in which you project a bad debt rate of 5 percent of credit sales. You might document this number as reasonable by referring to industry standards that show an industry average of 4 to 6 percent bad debt rates. The cash flow worksheet contained in this chapter provides a format for documenting many of the assumptions you will make, at least as they relate to your cash flow projections.

At the very least, your assumptions page should address the following items:

- The basis for your sales volume projections
- The number of employees needed to reach anticipated demand and how much they will cost you, including wages, payroll expenses, and benefits
- Your cost of goods sold
- Management salaries, if any, or owner withdrawals
- Key marketing expenses
- Major capital expenses
- Loans you project to add or retire and their (expected) interest rates

Finally, if you're pursuing financing, you should know that almost every financial institution will require that you provide a personal monthly expense summary (see the following worksheet) as well as personal financial statements, which will likely be completed on a form presented to you by the lender. These forms serve two primary purposes for the lender. The personal monthly expense sheet illustrates to the banker how much money you need to draw from the business on a monthly basis to meet your personal obligations and expenses. (It is also a good tool for you to use to ensure that the business will provide sufficient income to support your lifestyle.) The personal financial statement assists lenders with evaluating your creditworthiness and with identifying potential collateral that could be used to secure the loan.

PERSONAL MONTHLY EXPENSE SHEET

House payment or rent	$ ________
Maintenance and repair	$ ________
Food	$ ________
Clothing	$ ________
Utilities *(total of all, including phone and cable)*	$ ________
Auto loan payment 1	$ ________
Gasoline/Auto maintenance	$ ________
Insurance	$ ________
Taxes	$ ________
Credit cards	$ ________
Other loans *(list)*:	$ ________
Other loans *(list)*:	$ ________
Other loans *(list)*:	$ ________
Education	$ ________
Medical	$ ________
Entertainment/Travel	$ ________
Supplies	$ ________
Contributions	$ ________
Miscellaneous expenses	$ ________
Other expenses *(list)*:	$ ________
Other expenses *(list)*:	$ ________
Other expenses *(list)*:	$ ________
Total Monthly Personal Expenses	$ ________
Minus income from other sources	$ ________
Personal living expenses covered by the business	$ ________

Resource Directory

Appendix 1

Web Sites

www.sba.gov

The Small Business Administration has prepared an excellent site to assist the small business entrepreneur with information on loan guarantee programs, business plan development, marketing, and training. It also provides links to other important small business sites.

www.score.org

The Service Corps of Retired Executives (SCORE) is a volunteer organization sponsored by the Small Business Administration. SCORE was founded in 1964 to assist, counsel, and protect the interests of small business owners. It is a not-for-profit association and has a volunteer membership of over 12,000 retired business owners and corporate executives with experience to share.

www.onlinewbc.org

This site is specialized for women business owners. It offers information on business principles and practices, management techniques, and interactive mentoring and individual e-counseling. The North Texas Business Development Center prepared the site with the SBA's Women's Business Centers nationwide.

www.sba.gov/gcmed/index.html

The Small Business Administration Office of Minority Enterprise Development offers programs in business development, mentoring, and management and technical assistance to minority business owners.

www.asbdc-us.org

New and existing small business owners may take advantage of the free and confidential business counseling available through the Small Business Development Centers. This Web site helps you seek out your state and local SBDC offices. Simply call and set up an appointment to get training information, free one-to-one business counseling, and other resources for starting your business.

www.smallbizsmarts.com

This Web site provides the business owner with an interactive newsletter "that helps businesspeople maximize their profitability and reclaim their weekends."

www.smalloffice.com

Small business entrepreneurs can click their way to more resources and information related to business law, accounting, finance, and training opportunities.

www.isquare.com

Here you'll find the Small Business Adviser site. Within its Web pages are articles on business, tips on marketing, accounting information, and answers to your tax questions.

www.entreworld.org

A "quick-reference" site that you should bookmark. Formatted for end-user ease, this site is jam-packed with media resources, a business information center, a full business glossary, and hot links to other sites.

www.ideacafe.com

If you're wondering whether your business concept is worthwhile or has any merit, visit this site for feedback. You can sign up for contests; gain important, savvy advice on operating from home; or simply browse the site.

www.toolkit.cch.com

Compliance issues can be a complicated management concern. Utilizing this site may help you stay on top of current laws, provide you with ways to operate efficiently, show you how to save money, and help you obtain practical tips, business advice, legal information, and business tax information.

www.smallbusinesscenter.com

How's your credit? Visit this site and discover how to obtain your credit report. You can also learn about business loans, financing, and insurance.

www.homebusinessresearch.com

Here, you can explore tutorials, do research, uncover resources, and participate in forums.

www.iab.net

If e-commerce is in your future, check out the Internet Advertising Bureau, which features articles related to Internet commerce and Internet advertising.

www.inreach.com/sbdc/book/

See this site for "How to Start a Small Business," an online article that contains good basic information and adds validation to the business start-up process.

www.chamberbiz.com

Free registration provides you with access to this national chamber of commerce site. Here you'll find business news, information on government regulatory issues, marketing tips, and small business information.

Publications

With the explosion of new start-up enterprises, the demand for information has become intense. In response to that demand, books and magazines have appeared to assist business owners of every level.

Small Business Success Magazine

This publication offers useful articles on marketing, e-commerce, technology, business operations, and much more. Each issue has a specific theme and business focus. It's sponsored by the Small Business Administration, the Service Corp of Retired Executives, Pacific Bell, and other private-sector businesses. To obtain free copies of this magazine, call toll free, 800-848-8000. *Small Business Success* magazine is issued once per year and is generally released in the month of May.

The Small Business Financial Resource Guide

This guide includes a listing of federal and state government resources, information on financing options and process, descriptions of SBA loan guarantee programs, ratio information, and a glossary of accounting and financial terms. The publication is free, you pay for the postage and handling. To obtain a free copy, write to MasterCard International, c/o *The Small Business Financial Resource Guide*, 2000 Purchase Street, Purchase, NY 10577-2509.

Streetwise® Small Business Start-Up

The learning curve associated with being a new business owner can impair your potential success. Bring yourself up to speed on the start-up process, business development steps, business marketing concepts, and all aspects of starting a business with *Streetwise® Small Business Start-Up* by Bob Adams. Published by Adams Media Corporation in Avon, Massachusetts.

Streetwise® Customer-Focused Selling

Selling your product or service is critical to generating money for your business. Step off with confidence by learning the tricks of the trade with *Streetwise® Customer-Focused Selling* by Nancy J. Stephens with Bob Adams. Your cash flow may depend on it. Published by Adams Media Corporation in Avon, Massachusetts.

The SBA Loan Book

Business financing is one hurdle every entrepreneur dreads. With *The SBA Loan Book* by Charles Green, you'll breeze through the process with knowledge and assertiveness. No business should be without this book. It's the best hands-on, easy-to-understand text on the commercial loan process ever published. Published by Adams Media Corporation in Avon, Massachusetts.

1101 Businesses You Can Start from Home

If you're still in the dark as to what kind of a business to start, spend a few hours with *1101 Businesses You Can Start from Home* by Darly Allen Hall. This directory lists possible business to start–everything from remodeling to research is listed by category, with defining information and key points of consideration. Published by John Wiley and Sons, Inc. in New York City.

Barron's Business Law, 3rd Edition

Unless you're a lawyer, today's laws can be confusing. *Barron's Business Law* by Robert W. Emerson and John W. Hardwicke provides information, definitions, and key desktop references. Published by Barron's Educational Series, Inc. in Hauppauge, New York.

***Entrepreneur* Magazine**

A monthly publication offering information on small business topics, including e-commerce, advertising, and management. Available at the newsstand, by calling 800-274-6229, or at *www.entrepreneurmag.com.*

***American Demographics* Magazine**

This consumer-trends publication provides cutting-edge information on the markets you need to know about. Every issue offers business owners information on industry-specific trends–data essential to targeting and understanding your market. Available at the newsstand, by calling 800-529-7502, or by logging onto *www.demographics.com.*

Glossary

Appendix 2

This glossary has been developed to offer easy-to-understand definitions for complicated business terminology.

Accelerated repayment programs: Programs that help borrowers pay off loans faster, reducing the total interest paid over the term of the loan and allowing the borrower to build equity faster. A typical example of this repayment method is when a loan is repaid in twenty-four payments per year instead of twelve.

Accounting: A systematic method for keeping track of financial transactions. Accounting is used for tracking cash, assets, inventory, debt, expenses, and establishes the framework for interpreting the financial position of a business or individual. Accounting practices are directed by practice rules identified in the U.S. as "generally accepted accounting principles."

Accounts payable: Money owed to a supplier for products or services provided is referred to as accounts payable or vendor payables. This money is usually due within thirty days of receipt of the product or service. Accounts payable debt is recognized as unsecured debt and appears on the liability side (or the money owed side) of the balance sheet under "current liabilities." Types of common vendor payables include expenses for office supplies, gas and electric utilities, or advertising provided by telephone and newspaper publishers.

Accounts receivable: Customers who purchase goods and services on credit from your business are listed as an accounts receivable customer account, meaning that the goods or services were provided to the customer before payment was received. The time span between delivery of the goods or services and receipt of the customer's remittance is considered an accounts receivable.

Accruals: Financial transactions that are recorded on a financial statement but that remain unsettled as of the financial statement date.

Advertising: Activities executed by a business to promote sales. Advertising can take the form of a classified ad, a display ad, direct-mail items, radio or television commercials, signs, door-to-door canvassing, or any other activity intended to sell your product or service.

Application of funds: Loan applicants are usually required to file a written application of funds, a document identifying the intended use of the money to be borrowed. If the money borrowed is to be used to start a business, the application of funds could list uses like a building purchase, equipment and inventory purchases, and working capital.

Assets: Items that are owned, like cash, inventory, furniture and fixtures, vehicles, equipment, property, and loans made to others. While owning a building is an asset, a deposit paid to a utility company could also be considered an asset because the money will eventually be returned. Basically, an asset is anything you own that you could convert to cash to pay off debts. Assets are usually listed in order of liquidity.

B2B: Business-to-business selling.

B2C: Business-to-consumer selling.

B.A.I.L team: The B.A.I.L team is the group of professionals who provide support services to a business. The B.A.I.L team includes a banker, accountant, insurance agent, and lawyer.

Balance sheet: A report provided as part of a financial statement that acts as a "freeze frame" description of an individual's or business's financial position as of a given date. It lists total assets, total liabilities, and net worth.

Bookkeeping: A method of recording business transactions and reconciling business activities. Bookkeeping involves recording cash receipts, cash disbursements, sales, inventory, and purchases.

Break-even analysis: The calculated approximate sales volume required to cover costs, below which production would be unprofitable, and above which it would be profitable.

Business life cycle: The span of time between the beginning and the end of a business. Some businesses have a short life cycle, while others experience a long life. The manufacturer of the Stanley Steamer car had a short life, for example, while the Ford Motor Company has experienced a long life.

Business plan: A written document that describes the planned concept and execution of a business idea. The business plan includes information on the industry, the company's mission statement, its selected form of organization, local demographics, substantiated market research, planned marketing strategies, specific key personnel, financing requirements, financial projections, and professionals of record. The business plan is a progressive document that grows with the business.

Capacity: An ability to operate a business or repay a commercial loan with business revenues. Lenders review an entrepreneur's capacity to successfully meet the obligations of loan repayment.

Capital: The cash needed to start, operate, or grow a business. Usually, capital is the amount of cash invested by the business owner, venture capital firms, or private investors. When an infusion of capital is made into a business, it's usually given in exchange for a preestablished percentage of equity/ownership.

Cash flow: The movement of cash into the business from sales and accounts receivables and out of the business to pay expenses. Cash flow is a critical function in any business because cash is what pays the expenses. Positive cash flow is the state of having more cash flow into the business than is being paid out. Negative cash flow occurs when the amount of cash being paid out by the business exceeds that coming in. Negative cash flow is the number one reason businesses fail.

Clean-up: Commercial lines of credit may specify a thirty-day period in which the line-of-credit balance is to be paid in full. Usually this thirty-day period, which is called clean-up, comes after the line has been used for eleven months and is required for renewal of the line.

Collateral: Owned assets pledged to secure a loan. Equity owned in residential property, for example, is commonly used to secure a commercial loan.

Community Reinvestment Act: Congress enacted the Community Reinvestment Act (CRA) (12 U.S.C. 2901) in 1977 in an effort to encourage depository institutions to help meet the credit needs of the communities in which they operate, including low- and moderate-income neighborhoods. The CRA is implemented and monitored by Regulation BB (12 CFR 228) and was modified in May 1995. (For more information refer to *www.bog.frb.fed.us/DCCA/CRA/*).

Compliance: Establishing operational procedures and policies that meet regulatory requirements related to business operations. Check with federal, state, and local agencies to obtain compliance requirements.

Corporation: A form of organization that separates personal assets from business assets, providing liability protection for owners. Corporations have defined structures and are overseen by stockholders; a board of directors; and a president, vice president, secretary, and treasurer. A corporation is filed with a state's Department of State. Owners may elect to be a subchapter S corporation or a C corporation. Specific guidelines apply to each.

Cost of goods sold: The actual cost of items purchased for resale. The cost of goods sold is calculated by taking the inventory value at the beginning of an accounting period, adding the total amount of inventory purchases made during the period, and subtracting the ending inventory value, as follows:

Beginning inventory as of April 1, 2003	$1,000
Plus total inventory purchases	+ $500
Less ending inventory as of April 30, 2003	- $900
Cost of goods sold for April 2003	= $600

Credit criteria: Commercial lenders who originate loans use credit criteria to determine the credit worthiness of an applicant. There are five criteria for lending, know as the "Five Cs of Credit." They are cash, credit, collateral, capacity, and character. Additionally, credit criteria can include current economic conditions.

Credit report: An inclusive report of an individual's payment history that lists debts owed and paid, inquiries, judgments, and other financial information.

Credit reporting agencies: Organizations authorized to collect credit history information on individuals and businesses and summarize the findings in a report. Credit reporting agencies include Experian, TransUnion, Equifax, and Dun & Bradstreet. It is wise to obtain a credit report before requesting financing, so that any negative information can be addressed.

Credit scoring: A system for evaluating an individual's credit history. The Fair, Issac credit scoring process was developed to objectively and accurately rate financial repayment ability. ("Fair, Issac" refers to the names of the individuals who created the process.)

EBIT: Earnings before interest and taxes.

Economic Development Zones: Dedicated areas within a city or county in which businesses receive special benefits for being located. Benefits can include tax deferments, utility discounts, sales tax exemptions on building improvements, and tax credits for employee hiring. Call your local city or county economic development department for further details.

Entrepreneur: A special breed of individual who is willing to accept unavoidable risks to develop a business concept. Entrepreneurs possess a passion for business ownership.

Exit strategy: A preconceived plan for closing, selling, or transferring a business enterprise. Every business plan should include a well-thought-out exit strategy that creates a pathway for owners to leave the business.

Expenses: Operational costs incurred by a business enterprise. Expenses are noted on the profit and loss statement and may include advertising, loan interest, telephone services, electric services, office supplies, professional fees, rent, uniforms, wages, and other costs.

Fallback Position: An alternative plan for an activity. In business a good fallback position provides a safety net if an activity fails. Think "Plan B."

Financing: Obtaining a loan for personal or business purposes. Business financing is also known as commercial lending.

Grant: Money intended to help address a public need. Usually, the granting organization publishes a request for written grant proposals.

Gross profit: Profit before expenses and taxes. To calculate gross profit, determine the total amount of sales and subtract the cost of the product, freight, and other direct costs.

Inception balance sheet: A financial statement defining the financial position of a start-up business on the date the business opens.

Intangible assets: An asset that has value yet can't be physically touched. Business names are intangible assets.

Interest: A percentage of borrowed money paid to the lender. The annual percentage rate (APR) varies with a loan's amount and use. Higher-risk loans will be "margined" at a higher interest cost than lower-risk projects. New business start-ups are considered risky and usually carry a high rate of interest.

ISP: Internet service provider.

Lease: Contractual agreement between a property or equipment owner and the leasing individual. Leases are used for obtaining vehicles and equipment, retail and office space, and personnel.

Mail-order business: Creating sales and revenue through the mail as a result of direct-mail advertising activity. This type of business works well as a home-based business.

Marketing plan: A well-defined written plan for creating sales.

Niche: Specialized market segment where products and services address a specific need or demand. Sewing customized clothing for disabled people, for example, is a unique service and fulfills a niche market.

Personal loan guarantee: A signed written agreement that secures the borrower's personal responsibility for repayment of a loan or fulfillment of a lease agreement. Personal loan guarantees have become mandated and aggressively used to ensure recourse if default on a loan occurs. The savings and loan crisis in the late 1980s created a need to require more personal responsibility on the part of borrowers.

Prestart-up development: Planning and investigating a business concept. Prestart-up is the period before activities begin to open the business.

Profit and loss statement: One report found in a financial statement. The profit and loss statement documents sales, cost of goods sold, expenses, and net income before taxes.

Promotion: Educating the public about a product. Promotion is a bit different from advertising as it has more of an educational focus. For example, the American Dairy Association used promotion to discuss the health benefits of milk and dairy products in billboards and commercials before developing the advertising to sell milk, "Got milk?".

Risk: A measured and calculated probability of loan default. The lower the risk, the more likely a borrower will repay a debt. The higher the risk, the more unlikely the debt will be repaid. Business owners who need to borrow money should strive to be low-risk applicants.

Risk Management Association (RMA) annual statement studies: An association of more than 3,000 lending and credit risk professionals and includes commercial banks, thrift institutions, and U.S. financial institutions. RMA provides financial information by industry and offers analysis tools for considering loan risk. Small business owners may make use of this information when assessing a business venture. RMA strives to ensure current data, to improve practices and principles of commercial lending, and to help increase the profitability of its institutions. Check your local library for the annual studies.

SBA: Small Business Administration. The SBA is a federal economic development agency that provides loan guarantees to lending institutions to support higher-risk loans.

SBDC: Small Business Development Centers. The SBDCs are a national program funded by the SBA and financially supported by each state. The SBDCs provide free and confidential technical assistance to new and existing business owners.

SCORE: Service Corps of Retired Executives. This federal agency, funded by the SBA, is a volunteer group of retired business persons who provide training and support to business owners.

Secondary source of repayment: A planned and defined program for repaying debt should the primary sources of money become unavailable. If, for example, the business owner intends to repay debt with income from the business but the business fails, he or she should be able to turn to a second source of cash, such as employment, liquidating assets, or selling residential property to use for repayment.

Sources and uses: A document that defines the original source of cash for a business enterprise and describes how it will be utilized. Sources could include bank accounts, mutual funds, and gifts from relatives. Uses can include working capital, equipment purchases, building improvements, and advertising.

Sustainable rate of growth (SRG): The calculated rate at which a company can grow given certain conditions. Businesses that exceed their SRG and grow too fast will soon be bankrupt. The SRG is a gauge owners use to direct business growth activities. Growth requires cash. Businesses that grow faster than their cash will support usually fail.

Turnover ratios: A measurement of the number of times and the speed at which an operational cycle is completed. For example, inventory turnover ratios define the number of times a warehouse will sell and repurchase stock on the shelves. The higher the turnover ratio, the better the cash flow.